AN INTRODUCTION TO PRAYER
MUQADDIMAT AL-ṢALĀH

بِسۡمِ ٱللَّهِ ٱلرَّحۡمَٰنِ ٱلرَّحِيمِ

An Introduction to Prayer

Muqaddimat al-Ṣalāh

(Also known as *Khulāṣat al-Kaydānī*)

A Manual on the Rules of Prayer according to the Ḥanafī School of Jurisprudence

Luṭf Allāh al-Nasafī al-Kaydānī

Translation, Notes and Appendices
Siddiq A. Mitha

FIQHRA

First Edition, December 2021.

ISBN 978-1-9196531-0-5

Published by:
Fiqhra

Fiqhra Ltd, Bolton, UK
www.fiqhra.org
info@fiqhra.org

British Library Cataloguing in Publication Data. A catalogue record for this book is available from the British Library.

Printed by Mega Printing in Turkey

Book design, typography and cover design by Etherea Design

To
Dr Ṣalāḥ Abūl-Ḥājj,
a teacher whose passion,
dedication and knowledge
has inspired a generation

Contents

	INTRODUCTION	I
	LIST OF ABBREVIATIONS	VIII
	TRANSLITERATION KEY	IX
	HONORIFIC PHRASES	X
	The Arabic Text	1
	Author's Introduction	25
CHAPTER 1	The Obligatory	33
CHAPTER 2	The Necessary	39
CHAPTER 3	The Sunna	45
CHAPTER 4	The Recommended	51
CHAPTER 5	The Unlawful	55
CHAPTER 6	The Offensive	59
CHAPTER 7	The Permissible	69
CHAPTER 8	The Nullifiers	71
APPENDIX A	The Obligatory Components of Prayer and a Summary of Their Rulings	73
APPENDIX B	Supplications	75
	Bibliography	81
	About the Translator	87

Introduction

Our actions, in many ways, define who we are. They are physical manifestations of our beliefs and the values we hold dear, but more importantly, they can have consequences that ripple into the infinite world of the hereafter and dictate our ultimate fate. Thus, the actions we perform today are of indescribable significance.

Islam has placed great emphasis on action – merely believing is not sufficient to be eternally saved from the hellfire. Indeed, it is true that belief itself is not dependent upon action,[1] nor does the neglect of any act of devotion, generally speaking, strip one of faith.[2] However, it is still an integral part of what makes one a believer; it is evidence for the claim of faith, and it bears witness to our reality. The proof of our faith is in the life we have lived, which is nothing but the summation of our actions.

From the greatest of actions that a Muslim has been exhorted to perform is the *ṣalāh* or prayer. After accepting belief in Allah and His messenger, the adult believer must strive to establish the prayer in his life. The prayer is mentioned on multiple occasions in the Qur'an. Page after page includes references to 'establish the prayer',[3] either directly or indirectly. We are told to 'celebrate His glory in the evening and in the morning'[4] and 'in the late afternoon and at midday';[5] which correspond to the times of prayer. We are

---

1 Belief, according to the orthodox position of the Ahl al-Sunna, is achieved simply via its affirmation (*taṣdīq*) in one's heart. Acts of devotion are considered a perfecting condition (*sharṭ kamāl*), as opposed to the Mu'tazilites, who hold such acts to be a conditional component of belief (*Tuḥfat al-Murīd*, 95).

2 That is, as long as one does not deny its legislation, render that which is unlawful lawful or leave an act of devotion by way of disdain and contempt for the Sacred Law.

3 Q 2:43.

4 Q 30:17.

5 Q 30:18.

also taught 'to seek help through steadfastness and prayer'[6] and are reminded to keep it up, as it 'restrains outrageous and unacceptable behaviour'.[7]

The Prophetic traditions likewise describe the *ṣalāh* as 'light',[8] a criterion between faith and disbelief,[9] the 'first thing a slave will be asked about on the Day of Judgement'[10] and a 'pillar of the religion'.[11] In one narration the Messenger of Allah ﷺ describes the edifice of Islam as being built upon five things,[12] with the prayer being the second of these enumerated straight after the two testimonies of faith. Although, what is perhaps the greatest indication of the superiority of this act is the way in which it was revealed upon the Messenger of Allah ﷺ. Three years before the migration to Medina, the Messenger of Allah ﷺ was miraculously taken to Bayt al-Maqdis in Jerusalem, and it is there that he ﷺ ascended the heavens and communed with the Lord of the heavens and the earth. What is related from this event is that the Messenger of Allah ﷺ is gifted fifty prayers to perform each single day, which are eventually reduced to five by the advice of Mūsā. This makes *ṣalāh* the only act in Islam to be received by the Messenger ﷺ directly from Allah! This is no mere obligation, but in reality, it is a great blessing, an opportunity to commune with Allah Almighty, and this is why the prayer is so aptly described as the 'ascent of the believer' – an ascension in all its forms.

It is no wonder, then, that the scholars, sages and people of Allah were people of *ṣalāh*, prostrating and bowing before their Lord at every opportunity. It is reported that Zayn al-'Ābidīn 'Alī the son of Ḥusayn ﷺ would pray 1,000 supererogatory units of *ṣalāh* every single day.[13] Likewise, 'Abdullāh the son of Aḥmad b. Ḥanbal relates that his father would pray 300 supererogatory units each day.[14] The *ṣalāh* was sacred and the people of Allah knew it.

Its importance is manifest, but what is also vital to understand is that the *ṣalāh* is a well-defined act. It cannot be offered in any format one wishes; rather, its acceptance depends upon, like so many other actions, complete

---

6 Q 2:45.

7 Q 29:45.

8 *Muslim*, 1:203.223.

9 *Tirmidhī*, 5:13.261.

10 *Tirmidhī*, 1:269.413.

11 Suyūṭī in his *al-Jāmi' al-Ṣaghīr* (3:107) cites the source of this narration as being the *Shu'b al-Īmān* of Bayhaqī; and Ibn Ḥajar in *al-Talkhīṣ al-Ḥabīr* states, 'it has been narrated by Abū Nu'aym, the shaykh of Bukhārī, in the book of *ṣalāh*' (1:446).

12 *Bukhārī*, 1:11.8.

13 *al-'Ibar*, 1:83.

14 *Ḥilyat al-Awliyā'*, 9:181.

adherence to the way of the Messenger of Allah ﷺ. 'Pray like you see me praying,'[15] commanded the Messenger of Allah ﷺ – an indication that the prayer has an outward dimension that one is obliged to fulfil for its validity. Thus, the jurists from the very early period of Islam began to elucidate and clarify the prayer of the Messenger of Allah ﷺ.

There is no real disagreement with regards to the general format of prayer. All scholars agreed that one must recite, bow and prostrate, but naturally, certain aspects of the prayer were not definite. Should one say '*Āmīn*' loudly? Is the recital of the Fātiḥa obligatory? Where do you place the hands when reciting in the standing position? These ancillary matters were the domain of the *fuqahā'*. Author-jurists (*mujtahidūn*) had to use their knowledge, acumen and insight to perform *ijtihād* and extrapolate what they felt best represented the prayer of the Messenger of Allah ﷺ.

The school of Kufa, led by the great Imam Abū Ḥanīfa, did just that. It clarified, according to its principles, what it felt best described the prayer of the Messenger of Allah ﷺ. The rulings surrounding prayer, however, over time continually developed as the scholars were faced with new and complex scenarios: How should you pray if you can't recite Arabic? Or what do you do if you forget to recite a sura or perform an extra prostration? Thus, the scholars penned works and treatises to clarify these rulings, many of which were extrapolations (*takhrījāt*) from the understandings of the early author-jurists. As more and more details were added, and the discussions became longer and complicated, the need for short, succinct and palatable works arose.

The *Muqaddimat al-Ṣalāh* is one such tract. It is neither complex nor long, but it is actually its brevity and simplicity that gives it its immense worth. This is a book that gained much acceptance[16] and is still studied widely in seminaries all around the Indian subcontinent and in institutions around the world that affiliate with the Ḥanafī school. The author's systematic approach and inclusion of intricate and detailed rulings – which are rarely found in even some longer and more expansive works[17] – makes it a valuable resource for the beginner looking to learn how to perform *ṣalāh* and delve into the codification of rulings according to the school of Abū Ḥanīfa. Its importance as a manual is also attested to by many scholars, such as

15 *Bukhārī*, 1:226.605.

16 Quhustānī is reported to have said, 'It [the book] has spread like the spreading of [the rays of] the sun in broad daylight, in [the lands of] Transoxiana (*mā warā al-nahr*)' (*Kashf al-Ẓunūn*, 2:1802).

17 Ibrāhīm al-Bukhārī states, 'it – even with its extreme brevity – comprises important rulings that the people need, and [with it one] can dispense of a hundred [other] common works' (*Kashf al-Ẓunūn*, 2:1802).

Ṭāshkubrī Zāda, Quhustānī, ʿAbd al-Ghanī al-Nābulsī, Mīr Darvīsh al-Bukhārī and Aqḥaṣārī, who penned commentaries upon this work.

A NOTE ON THE TRANSLATION AND COMMENTARY

I had the opportunity of studying this work in 2020, in Amman, Jordan, with my beloved and esteemed teacher Dr Ṣalāḥ Abūl-Ḥājj and thereafter was blessed to receive an *ijāza* to teach the work. Although I was previously familiar with the book, I only came to understand its true value after studying it. I did not, however, have the intention to translate the work, but upon the request of my teacher Dr Ṣalāḥ – may Allah preserve him – I set out to do so for an English audience.

One of the most detrimental things a beginner student of fiqh can do is to get bogged down by detail and legal evidences, and so, this tract and others like it are extremely beneficial to learn in order to gain an initial framework of a certain topic in fiqh – in this case the prayer. After grounding oneself, one can slowly build upon prior knowledge; however, it is important that what one is building upon be sound and reliable in its representation of the school. Generally, the earlier scholars and their works are better at providing a strong and reliable framework as they keep closer to the original positions of the school. And this is why, even though there may be later or more contemporary works that outline for us prayer in a more detailed and organised manner, studying them first as a student of knowledge, in my humble opinion, is a flaw. Also, tracts like the present work are great at offering a vista unto how the earlier Imams understood certain topics; for example, in this work one sees how the author feels about raising the finger in *tashahhud*. These issues are brilliant in providing an understanding of the differences between the scholars in the school and create a gateway to learn that the madhhab is an intricate framework full of discussion and debate.

At the start of the book, the author deals with the categorisation and definition of rulings in the school. This is an extremely important topic as it forms the basis for understanding issues in any topic in fiqh. A student must learn to place things in their correct place so as not to fall into unwanted rigidity – which is currently rampant – or to make difficult that which has been made easy and vice versa. Determining how to do this begins with learning the categorisation of rulings and how to differentiate between them properly – something which may seem simple but is quite complex in reality.

I have tried to elaborate, explain and clarify, where appropriate, the author's words by mostly consulting the commentaries of ʿAbd al-Ghanī al-Nābulsī, *al-Jawhar al-Kullī*, which I found extremely useful and to the point on many issues, and Dr Ṣalāḥ, *al-Mirqāt*, which is as usual packed with indispensable information. Where necessary, I have used other works in the school to add more depth or clarity. This is not a work of evidence (*istidlāl*) and so, the 'why' something is a certain way was not my objective in the commentary. However, any Qur'anic verses or hadiths pertaining to a matter are generally cited as a way of connecting the reader with the Qur'an and Sunna. For economy of space, references in the notes are provided in short form (see the Bibliography for full publication details), while oft-cited works are summarised in the List of Abbreviations. Hadith citations are given in the format '*Muslim*, 1:203.223', meaning, in this example, volume 1, page 203 and hadith number 223 (in that order) of Muslim's *Ṣaḥīḥ*.

With regards to the translation, I have made use of *al-Mirqāt*, which includes an edited version of the original manuscript of the text alongside its commentary produced by Dr Ṣalāḥ and published by Dār al-Fatḥ in Amman, Jordan. I chose to translate the Arabic of the treatise from this edition primarily because it was the one I studied myself. It must be noted, however, that there are multiple editions of this work in print, and one may find slight variances in the others when compared with the Arabic text presented here.

The Arabic includes chapter titles, but for purposes of greater clarity and ease, I have interpolated some subheadings and organised the rulings in list form.

THE AUTHOR

As mentioned, this tract is a renowned work, but, surprisingly, there is no consensus with regards to its author. The more well-known opinion and what is prevalent amongst the common folk is that it is the work of Luṭf Allāh al-Nasafī (d. 900 AH), better known as al-Fāḍil al-Kaydānī. 'Abd al-Ghanī al-Nābulsī, Quhustānī, Mīr Darvīsh al-Bukhārī and Ibrāhīm Bāshā all corroborate this in their commentaries. However, Ḥājjī Khalīfa in his bibliographic encyclopaedia, *Kashf al-Ẓunūn*, attributes it to Shams al-Dīn al-Fanārī (d. 834 AH) and states, 'This is what is correct.' Ṭāshkubrī Zāda, unlike the other commentators, seems to agree with Ḥājjī Khalīfa. The third person it has been attributed to, by Ḥasan al-Kāfī al-Aqḥasārī, is Ibn Kamāl Bāshā (d. 940 AH), the well-known jurist of the Ottoman Empire. All in all, I have chosen to attribute it to Luṭf Allāh al-Nasafī al-Kaydānī simply because this is what is most prevalent and accepted with regards to the authorship of this tract.

THE TITLE OF THE WORK

Similarly, like the author of the work, there is much dispute with regards to its title. It has been called *Muqaddimat al-Ṣalāh* by Ḥājjī Khalīfa, *ʿUmdat al-Muṣallī* by ʿAbd al-Ghanī al-Nābulsī, *Khulāṣat al-Kaydānī* generally by the scholars from the Indian subcontinent, *al-Muqaddima al-Kaydāniyya* by Quhustānī and *Maṭālib al-Muṣallī* by the Aal al-Bayt Catalogue of Arab Islamic Manuscripts. It is difficult therefore to ascertain what its actual name may be, and so I have chosen to call it *Muqaddimat al-Ṣalāh* as it is the clearest and the name which Dr Ṣalāḥ preferred for his edition of the book.

THE JURISTIC GRADE OF THE BOOK

Without doubt this tract has gained wide repute and has been given much attention by the scholars; however, it is still considered an 'unreliable' (*ghayr muʿtabar*) book according to the Ḥanafī jurists, as has been explicitly mentioned by Laknawī[18] and others.[19] The cause for its unreliability is most likely due to the ambiguity of its author and in ascertaining his level of scholarship (i.e. if we consider its author to be Luṭf Allāh al-Nasafī) and the inclusion of certain issues in the chapter of the unlawful which are generally accepted as not being unlawful. This is why it is important that this book is studied with a commentary, and its rulings are compared and checked with some of the more reliable works of the school so one is aware of which rulings need rectifying or are in need of further explanation. If this text *is* read in this manner, then the causes of its unreliability are no doubt removed and in fact it becomes a primer of great value.[20]

It is hoped that this work infuses in its readers a sincere love for prayer and becomes a beneficial guide for the student of Ḥanafī fiqh. Any discrepancies and mistakes are my own, and any good in this work is from the grace of

18 *ʿUmdat al-Riʿāya*, 1:57 (introduction).

19 *Uṣūl al-Iftā*, 209.

20 It is important to note that the objective of studying a book that has been chosen as part of a traditional curriculum is not necessarily for the acquisition of the 'right' answer, but it is to train a student's faculty of reasoning and acumen in that particular science such that he learns *how* to arrive at the right answer. When a book is chosen for study, one can find an accumulation of commentaries and scholarly debate that discuss the rulings in detail which ultimately presents the student a vast array of information and knowledge, which in turn helps him to understand a great deal in a short space of time. This is why, even though other books may be stronger or better than the present work in giving the 'right' answer, this book has been studied, and continues to be studied, by scholars and students till this day.

Allah alone. All praise is due to Allah, and may salutations and peace be upon Muhammad ﷺ, his pure family and noble Companions.

ABBREVIATIONS

Abū Dāwūd	*Sunan Abī Dawūd*
Badā'i'	Kāsānī's *Badā'i' al-Ṣanā'i'*, a commentary on 'Alā' al-Dīn al-Samarqandī's *Tuḥfat al-Fuqahā'*
Bahr	Zayn al-Din Ibn Nujaym's *al-Bahr al-Ra'iq*, a commentary on *Nasafi's Kanz al-Daqa'iq*
Bukhārī	*Ṣaḥīḥ al-Bukhārī*
Durr	Ḥaṣkafī's *al-Durr al-Mukhtār*, a commentary on Tumurtāshī's *Tanwīr al-Abṣār*
Fatḥ	Ibn al-Humām's supercommentary on Marghīnānī's *Hidāya*
Ḥalabī Kabīr	Ibrāhīm al-Ḥalabī's *Ghunyat al-Mutamallī*, a commentary on Kāshgharī's *Munyat al-Muṣallī*
Jawhar	'Abd al-Ghanī al-Nābulsī's *al-Jawhar al-Kullī*, a commentary on Kaydānī's *Muqaddimat al-Ṣalāh*
Marāqī	Shurunbulālī's *Marāqī al-Falāḥ*, a commentary on his *Nūr al-Īḍāḥ*
Minḥa	'Aynī's *Minḥat al-Sulūk*, a commentary on Rāzī's *Tuḥfat al-Mulūk*
Munya	Kāshgharī's *Munyat al-Muṣallī wa-Ghunyat al-Mubtadī*
Muslim	*Ṣaḥīḥ Muslim*
Radd	Ibn 'Ābidīn's *Radd al-Muḥtār* (*Ḥāshiyat Ibn 'Ābidīn*), a supercommentary on Ḥaṣkafī's *al-Durr al-Mukhtār*
Ṣāḥibayn	Abū Yūsuf Ya'qūb b. Ibrāhīm and Muhammad b. al-Ḥasan al-Shaybānī, the two foremost students of Abū Ḥanīfa
Tabyīn	Zayla'ī's *Tabyīn al-Ḥaqā'iq*, a commentary on Nasafī's *Kanz al-Daqā'iq*
Tanwīr	Tumurtāshī's *Tanwīr al-Abṣār*
Tirmidhī	*Sunan al-Tirmidhī*
Tuḥfa	Zayn al-Dīn al-Rāzī's *Tuḥfat al-Mulūk*

TRANSLITERATION KEY

ء(إأ)	‘	ض	ḍ
ا	a, ā	ط	ṭ
ب	b	ظ	ẓ
ت	t	ع	a, ‘i, ‘u’ ,’
ث	th	غ	gh
ج	j	ف	f
ح	ḥ	ق	q
خ	kh	ك	k
د	d	ل	l
ذ	dh	م	m
ر	r	ن	n
ز	z	ه	h
س	s	و	w, u, ū
ش	sh	ي	y, i, ī
ص	ṣ		

HONORIFIC PHRASES

'Azza wa-jalla	Mighty and Sublime
Ṣalla Allāh 'alayhi wa-sallam	may Allah bless him and give him peace
'Alayhi al-salām	peace be upon him
'Alayhim al-salām	peace be upon them
'Alayhā al-salām	peace be upon her
Raḍī Allāh 'anhu	may Allah be pleased with him
Raḍī Allāh 'anhumā	may Allah be pleased with them both
Raḍī Allāh 'anhum	may Allah be pleased with them
Raḍī Allāh 'anhā	may Allah be pleased with her

But say, 'Lord, increase me in knowledge!'

Q 20:114

مُقَدِّمَة الصّلاَة

المنسوبة إلى

لطف الله النسفي الكيداني

بِسْمِ ٱللَّهِ ٱلرَّحْمَٰنِ ٱلرَّحِيمِ

الحمدُ لله ربّ العالمين، والعاقبةُ للمتّقين، والصلاةُ والسّلامُ عَلى رسولِهِ محمّد، وآلِهِ أجمعين.

اِعْلَمْ بأنّ العبدَ مُبتلىً بين أن يُطيعَ اللهَ تعالى فيُثاب، وبين أَن يَعْصِيَه فيُعاقَب، والْاِبتلاءُ يتعلّق بالمشروعِ وغيرِ المشروع، فعلاً وتركاً، فلا بُدَّ مِنْ بيانِ أنواعِ المشرُوعاتِ وغيرِ المشروعاتِ، وبيانِ معانيها وأحكامِها؛ لِيَسْهُلَ على الطالبِ دركُها وضبطُها. فنقولُ وبالله التوفيق:

المشروع [أنواعٌ] أربعة:

١. فرض
٢. وواجب
٣. وسنّة
٤. ويليها المباح

وغيرُ المشروع نوعان:

١. مُحَرَّم
٢. ومكرُوه

ويتلوهما: المفسِدُ للعمل المشروعِ فيه.

أمّا الفرضُ: فما ثَبَتَ بدليلٍ قطعيٍّ لا شبهةَ فيه.
وحكمُه: الثوابُ بالفعل، والعقابُ بالتّرك بلا عذْرٍ، والكفرُ بالإنكار في المتّفقِ عليه.

والواجبُ: ما ثَبَتَ بدليلٍ فيه شبهة.
وحكمُه: كحكمِ الفرض عملاً لا اعتقاداً، حتّى لا يُكفَرُ جاحِدُه.

والسّنّة: ما واظبَ عليه النّبيُّ ﷺ مع تركِه مرّةً أو مرّتَين.
وحكمُه: الثّواب بالفعل، والعتابُ بالتّرك في سنّةِ الهُدى.

والمستحَبُّ: ما فَعَلَه النّبيُّ ﷺ مرّةً وترَكَه مرةً أخرى، وما أحبَّه السَّلفُ.
وحكمُه: الثَّوابُ بالفعلِ وعَدَمُ العتابِ بالتَّرك.

والمباح: ما يُخيَّر العبدُ فيه بين الإتيان والتَّرك.
وحكمُه: عدمُ الثَّواب والعقاب فعلاً وتركًا.

والمحرّم: ما ثَبَتَ بالنّهيِ بلا معارِضٍ له
وحكمُه: الثَّواب بالتَّرك لله عزّ وجلّ، والعقابُ بالفعل، والكفرُ بالاستِحْلالِ في المتَّفقِ عليه.

والمكروه: ما ثَبَتَ النّهيُ فيه مع المعارِض.
وحكمُه: الثّوابُ بالتّرك الموصوف، وخوفُ العقابِ بالفعل، وعَدَمُ الكفرِ بالاستحلال.

والمفسدُ: هو النّاقضُ للعمل المشروعِ فيه.

وحكمُه: العقاب بالفعل عمدًا وعدمُه سهواً.

ثم اعلَمْ بأنّ الصّلاةَ جامعةً للأربعة الأُوَلِ شرعاً، وقد تُوجد الأربعةُ الأخيرةُ فيها طبعاً.

فلا بدّ مِنْ تفصيل كلِّ نوعٍ وتِعدادِها بطريق الانحِصارِ والاختصارِ مرتّباً على ثمانيةِ أبوابٍ تيسيراً للمُؤمنين.

الباب الأوَّل

في بيانِ الفَرائض

وهي خمسةَ عشرَ، بعضُها خارجيّة، وبعضُها داخِليَّة.

أمّا الخارجيةُ، فثمانية:

١. الوقتُ.
٢. وطهارةُ البَدَن.
٣. والثّوب
٤. والمَكان.
٥. وستْرُ العَوْرة.
٦. واسْتِقبالُ القِبلة.
٧. والنِّيَّة.
٨. والتَّكبيرةُ الأُولى.

وأما الدّاخلية، فسبعةٌ:

١. القِيام.
٢. والقِراءة.
٣. والرُّكوع.
٤. والسُّجود.

٥. والقَعْدةُ الأخيرة.

٦. والتَّرتيبُ فيما اتَّحَدَتْ شرعِيَّتُهُ في كلِّ ركعةٍ، أو في جميعِ الصَّلاة.

٧. والخروجُ بفعلِ المصلِّي.

البابُ الثّاني

في الواجبات

وهي إحدى وعشرون.

منها: ما يعُمّ جميعَ المصلّين وجميعَ الصَّلواتِ، وهي سبعةٌ.

ومنها ما يخُصُّ بعضَ المصلّين وبعضَ الصّلاة، وهي أربعةَ عشرَ.

أمّا العامّ:

١. فلفظُ التَّكبيرِ للتَّحريمة.
٢. والقَعْدَةُ الأُولى.
٣. والتّشَهُّد في القَعْدَتين.
٤. والطُّمَأْنِينَةُ في الرُّكوعِ والسُّجود.
٥. وإتيانُ كلِّ فرضٍ في موضِعِه.
٦. وإتيانُ كلِّ واجبٍ كذلك.
٧. والخروجُ بلفظِ السَّلام.

وأمّا الخاصُّ:

١. فتَعْيينُ الأُولَيَيْن للقراءة.
٢. والفاتحةُ لهما.
٣. واقتصارُها على مرّة.

٤. وضَمُّ سورةٍ، أو ثلاثِ آياتٍ قصيرةٍ، أو آيةٍ طويلةٍ معها.

٥. وتقديمُ الفاتحةِ عليها.

وهذه من عليه القراءةُ.

٦. والقُنُوتُ في الوِتْر.

٧. والجَهْرُ في موضعِه جماعةً.

٨. والمخافَتَةُ كذلك.

٩. وإنصاتُ المقتدِي وقتَ قراءةِ الإمام.

١٠. ومتابعةُ الإمامِ على أيِّ حالٍ وَجَدَه، وإنْ لم يكنْ محسوباً مِنْ صلاتِهِ.

١١. وسجدةُ التِّلاوةِ على الإمام والمنفَرِدِ.

١٢. وتكبِيراتُ العِيدَينِ.

١٣. وتكبيرُ ركوعهما.

١٤. وسجودُ السَّهوِ على الإمام والمنفرِد بترْكِهِ واجباً في الصُّور الثَّمانيةِ الأُوَلِ مِنَ القِسْمِ الأَخيرِ، وفي جميع الصُّور مِنَ القسم الأَوّل إلا الطُّمأْنينة؛ فإنّها واجبةٌ للغير.

البابُ الثّالث

في السُّنن

وهي سبعةٌ وعِشرون.

العامّ منها: سبعةَ عشرَ، وهي:

١. رفْعُ اليدَينِ في التَّحريمةِ.

٢. وفي القُنوتِ.

٣. وفي تكبيراتِ العِيدَينِ.

٤. ونشْرُ الأصابعِ ثَمَّ.

٥. والثَّناء.

٦. ووَضْعُ اليُمنى على الشِّمال.

٧. وتكبيراتُ الانتقالاتِ حتّى القُنوتِ.

٨. وتسبيحُ الرّكوع ثلاثاً.

٩. وأخْذُ رُكبَتَيه في الرّكوع.

١٠. وتفريج الأصابعِ فيه.

١١. والقَوْمة.

١٢. والجلسة.

١٣. والسَّجدةُ على سبعةِ أعضاء.

١٤. وتسبيحُ السُّجود ثلاثاً.

١٥. والصلاةُ على النَبيِّ ﷺ بعد تَشَهُّدِ السّلام.

١٦. والدُّعاء بعده لنفسه ولجميعِ المؤمنين.

١٧. والسَّلامُ يمُنةً ويُسرةً.

والخاصّ، عَشَرة:

١. جهْر الإمامِ بالتَّكبيرات.

١. ومُقارنةُ المقتدي تكبيرةَ الإمام.

٢. ومتابعتُه له في سائرِ أفعالِهِ.

٣. والتعوُّذ.

٤. وإخفاؤُه.

٥. والتَّسميةُ بعده.

٦. وإخفاؤُها.

٧. وهذه الأربعةُ للإمام والمنفرِد.

٨. والتأمينُ سراً لهما، وللمقتدي في الجهرية.

٩. والتَّسميع للإمام، والتَّحميدُ للمقتدي، وللمنفردِ الجمعُ في أيِّ صلاةٍ.

١٠. وافتراشُ رِجْلِه اليُسرى لِلْجُلُوسِ عليها مَعَ نَصْبِ اليُمنى في القَعْدةِ لِلرِّجال، ولِلنِّساء التَوَرُّك.

البابُ الرّابع

في المستَحَبّات

وهي ثلاثةٌ وعِشرُون.

العامُّ، أربعةَ عشرَ:

١. تَرْكُ الإلْتِفاتِ يميناً وشِمالاً، كما قيل.

٢. وتَغْطِيةُ الفمِ عند التَّثاؤُب.

٣. ودفعُ السُّعالِ ما اسْتَطاعَ.

٤. وزِيادةُ القراءةِ على ثلاثِ آياتٍ.

٥. وتَرْتيلُ القراءةِ.

٦. وتَسْويةُ الرَّأسِ مع الظَّهرِ في الرُّكُوعِ.

٧. وَوَضْعُ رُكبتَيه قبلَ يدَيه، ووَضْعُ يدَيه قبل الأَنفِ، والأَنْفُ قبل الجَبْهَة لِلسُّجودِ.

٨. وعلى عكسِ ذلك الرَّفعُ لِلقِيامِ.

٩. والسُّجودُ بين اليدَينِ.

١٠. وتوجيهُ أصابعَ يدَيْه ورِجلَيه نحوَ القِبلةِ.

١١. وتَرْكُ مَسحِ الجبهةِ مِنَ التُّرابِ والعَرَقِ قبل السّلامِ.

١٢. والفَصْلُ بين القَدَمين قَدْرَ أربعةِ أصابعَ في القيامِ.

١٣. ووضْعُ يدَيه على فَخِذَيه في القَعْدَةِ.

١٤. وتحويلُ وجهِهِ يمُنةً ويُسرةً عندَ السّلامِ.

والخاصّ، تسعةٌ:

١. رَفعُ يدَيْه فيما سُنَّ حِذاءَ شَحْمَتَيْه للرِّجالِ، وحذاءَ المَنْكِبِ للنِّساءِ.

٢. ووَضْعُ اليدَينِ تحتَ السُّرّةِ للرِّجال، وعلى الصَّدْرِ للنِّساء.

٣. وإخراجُ الكَفَّينِ مِنَ الكُمَّين عندَ التَّحريمةِ للرِّجال.

٤. والقراءةُ على القَدْرِ المرويِّ للإمام.

٥. وزيادةُ التَّسبيحاتِ على الثَّلاثِ وتراً للمُنفرِدِ.

٦. وإبعادُ الضَّبْعَينِ مِنَ البطنِ، والبطنُ مِنَ الفَخِذِ، والفَخِذُ مِنَ السّاقِ، والسّاق مِنَ الأرضِ في السّجودِ للرِّجال، وبالعكس للنِّساء.

٧. وقراءةُ الفاتحةِ بعدَ الأُولَيَين للمفترِضِ في المشهُورِ.

٨. والتَّسْميةُ قبلَ الفاتحةِ في كُلِّ رَكْعةٍ.

٩. وانْتِظارُ المسبوقِ فراغَ الإمامِ.

البابُ الخامس

في المحَرَّمات

وهي أربعةَ عشرَ على العُموم:

١. الجهرُ بالتَّسْمِيةِ.
٢. والجهرُ بالتَّأمين.
٣. والالتفاتُ يميناً وشمالاً بتحويلِ بعضِ الوجهِ.
٤. والنَّظَرُ إلى السَّماءِ.
٥. والاتِّكاءُ على أسطوانةٍ أو اليدِ ونحوهما بلا عذرٍ.
٦. ورفعُ اليدَينِ في غير ما شُرِعَ.
٧. ورَفْعُ الأصابعِ في الرُّكوعِ والسُّجودِ عنِ الأرضِ.
٨. والجلوسُ على عَقِبَيه للتَّشَهُّدِ.
٩. والعَبَثُ بثوبِهِ، أو بَدَنِه دون الثَّلاث.
١٠. والإشارةُ بالسَّبابةِ كأهلِ الحديثِ.
١١. وقَصْرُ السَّلامِ على جانبٍ واحدٍ.
١٢. والقُنوتُ في غيرِ الوترِ.
١٣. والزيادةُ في التَّكبيرِ، أو الثَّناءِ، أو التَّسبيحاتِ، أو التَّشَهُّدِ على السُّنَّةِ.
١٤. وتَرْكُ الواجِبِ ممّا سَبَقَ عمداً، وفي «المحيط» ذُكِرتِ المحرَّماتِ في المكرُوهاتِ.

البابُ السّادس

في المكروهاتِ التي تُكرَه في الصّلاة

وهي تسعةٌ وخمسون.

العامُّ، اثنان وأربعون:

١. تكرارُ التّكبير.

٢. والعَدّ باليد للآي، ونحوِهما.

٣. والتَّخَصُّر.

٤. وما هو مِنْ أخلاقِ الجبابرة.

٥. والتّنَحْنُح بلا عذرٍ لو بغير حروف.

٦. والتنَخُّم.

٧. والنَّفْخُ غيرُ المسموع.

٨. وإمساكُ الدَّراهمِ ونحوها في الفم بحيث لا يمنعُ القراءة.

٩. وإعلاءُ الرّأسِ في الرّكوع.

١٠. وابتلاع ما بين الأسنانِ لو كان قليلاً.

١١. وترْكُ سنّةٍ مِنَ السّنن.

١٢. وإتمامُ القراءةِ في الرّكوع.

١٣. وتحصيلُ الأذكارِ في الانتقالات.

١٤. ووَضْعُ يَدَيه قبل رُكبَتَيه على الأرضِ للسُّجُود بلا عذرٍ.

١٥. ورفعهما بعدَ رُكبتيه للقيام كذلك.

١٦. والإقعاءُ كإقعاءِ الكلب.
١٧. وتغطيةُ الفم بلا غلَبة التثاؤب.
١٨. وغمْضُ العينَين.
١٩. وقلْبُ الحصى إلا أن لا يمكنُه السجودَ فأتى به مرّةً أو مرّتَين.
٢٠. ومسْحُ جبهتِه عن التُّراب أو العَرَقِ قبل الفراغ.
٢١. وكفُّ الثوب.
٢٢. والتّثاؤب.
٢٣. والتَّمطِّي.
٢٤. وفرْقَعَةُ الأصابع.
٢٥. والاستراحة مِنْ رِجْلٍ إلى رِجْل.
٢٦. وتفريجُ الأصابِعِ في غير الرّكوع.
٢٧. والتَّعجيل في القراءة.
٢٨. وترْكُ تسويةِ الرّأسِ مع الظَّهْرِ راكعاً.
٢٩. والتَّخَطِّي ثلاثاً فصاعداً بلا عذرٍ لو وقف بعد كلِّ خطوة.
٣٠. والتَّمايلُ يميناً وشمالاً.
٣١. وقتْلُ القَمْلَةِ دون الثّلاث.
٣٢. ودفْنُها كذلك.
٣٣. وإلقاءُ البُزاقِ.
٣٤. ونَزْعُ الخُفِّ بعملٍ قليلٍ.
٣٥. وشَمُّ الطِّيب.
٣٦. والتَّرَوُّحُ بالثّوب والمِرْوحةِ دون الثّلاث.
٣٧. وتعْيين السُّورةِ لصلاةٍ معيَّنةٍ بحيث لا يَقرَأُ غيرَها.
٣٨. والجمْعُ بين السّورتَين بتَرْك واحدةٍ بينهما في ركعةٍ واحدةٍ.

٣٩. والانتقالُ مِن آية إلى آية أخرى ولو كان بينهما سورة.
٤٠. وتقديمُ السّورةِ المتأخرةِ على المتقدمة، ولو في الرَّكعتَين.
٤١. والتّسمية قبل كلِّ سورةٍ في كلِّ ركعةٍ.
٤٢. وحَمْلُ الصَّبيِّ بلا عذرٍ.

والخاصُّ، سبعةَ عشرَ:

١. انتظارُ الإمامِ لِمن سَمِعَ خَفْقَ نعْلَيه للصّلاة.
٢. وتَطْويلُ الثّانيةِ على الأُولى في الفرائض.
٣. والتّوقُّفُ في آية الرّحمة والعذاب للإمام والمقتدي مطلقاً، وللمنفرد في الفرائض.
٤. والسَّجدةُ على كَوْرِ العِمامةِ.
٥. وإلصاقُ البطْنِ بالفخذِ للرِّجال.
٦. وكذلك بسْطُهم العَضُدَيْن.
٧. ونزْعُهم القميصَ أو القَلَنْسُوَةِ، ولُبْسُهم كذلك بعَمَلٍ يَسِيرٍ.
٨. وتَطْويلُ الإمامِ للصَّلاةِ بحيث يثقُلُ على القوم.
٩. وتخفيفُه لها لعَجَلَتِهم.
١٠. وإلجاءُ الإمام القومَ للفتحِ إذا قرأ ما يجوزُ به الصَّلاةَ.
١١. وجهْرُ القراءةِ في نوافل النَّهارِ.
١٢. وقراءةُ الإمامِ آيةَ السَّجدةِ فيما يُخافتُ إلا في آخِرِ السُّورة.
١٣. وتكرارُ الآيةِ سُروراً أو حُزْناً في الفرائضِ بلا عذرٍ، إلا في النَّوافلِ والسُّننِ المطْلقة.
١٤. وتكرارُ السُّورةِ في ركعةٍ واحدةٍ في الفرائض.
١٥. والصَّلاةُ رافعاً كُمَّيْه إلى المِرفقين للرِّجال.

١٦. وقولُ المُقتدِي عندَ آيةِ التّرغيبِ والتَّرهيب: صَدَقَ اللهُ تعالى وبلَّغَتْ رُسُلُه.

١٧. والاعتمادُ بحائطٍ أو أسطوانةٍ ونحوِها بلا عذرٍ في غيرِ النَّوافل.

البابُ السّابع

في المُباحات

وهي أحدَ عشرَ.

العامُّ، ثمانيةٌ:

١. نظْرُه بمُوقِ عَينَيْه بلا تحويلِ وجهِهِ.
٢. وتسويةُ موضعِ سجودهِ مرّةً أو مرّتَين للعذرِ.
٣. وقتلُ الحيّةِ المطْلقةِ مطلقاً، وإنْ احتاح إلى المعالجةِ.
٤. وفي فمِهِ دراهمُ أو دنانيرُ بحيث لا يمنعُه عن سُنّةِ القراءةِ.
٥. وفي يدِه ما لا يمنعُ عن سنّةِ الاعتمادِ.
٦. وقراءةُ القرآنِ على التأليف.
٧. ونَفْضُ الثّوب كيلا يلْتَصِقُ بجَسَدِه في الرُّكوع.
٨. وقراءةُ آخِرِ سورةٍ في ركعةٍ، وآخِرِ أُخرى في أُخرى على الصّحيح.

والخاصُّ، ثلاثةٌ:

١. تكرارُ السُّورةِ في ركعةٍ في التَّطوُّع.
٢. وأن يكونَ مُعْتَمِداً حائطاً أو أسطوانةً في التَّطوُّع ولو بلا عذرٍ.
٣. ولحظُ الإمامِ إلى مَن خلْفَهُ شاكّاً ليقوم إنْ قام هو، ونحوه.

البابُ الثّامن

في المُفسِدات

وهي في التّحقيقِ خمسةٌ على العموم:

١. التّكلُّمُ بكلام النّاس مطلقاً حقيقةً أو حُكماً.
٢. والضّحِكُ.
٣. والعملُ الكثيرِ بلا إصلاحٍ.
٤. وترْكُ فرضٍ مِنَ الفرائضِ بلا عُذْرٍ، ولو طرَأَ فواتُهُ بدونِ اختيارِه.
٥. وتعمُّدُ الحدثِ.

Author's Introduction

In the Name of Allah, the Lord of Mercy, the Giver of Mercy

All praise is for Allah, the Lord of the Worlds, and the good end is for the pious. May salutations and peace be upon His messenger Muhammad ﷺ, upon his family and all his Companions.

Know that the slave is afflicted[21] between obeying Allah Almighty and in turn being rewarded, and between disobeying Him and in turn being punished.

This affliction is related to the legislated rulings [of the *sharīʿa*] and the non-legislated rulings that [respectively] concern the performance and non-performance [of an act].[22] And thus, it is incumbent to describe the [different] types of legislated and non-legislated rulings, their meanings and their legal consequences to make it easy for the student to understand them and learn them precisely.

Therefore, we say – and it is Allah who grants divine providence[23] – that legislated rulings are of four types:

1. The obligatory (*farḍ*)
2. The necessary (*wājib*)
3. The sunna
4. The recommended (*mustaḥabb*)

---

21 That is, to be tested by Allah. One should always be conscious of this fact and try to live in a way that gives life to this understanding at every moment. This concept is normally termed by the scholars of *taṣawwuf* as the station of *murāqaba* or the state of being constantly aware of the presence of Allah.

22 That is, one is tested with performing the legislated rulings like *ṣalāh* or fasting, and neglecting the non-legislated rulings like avoiding fornication or alcohol.

23 Divine providence or *tawfīq* is to create in the slave the ability to perform acts of obedience, as opposed to *khidhlān* or being forsaken, which is the opposite of *tawfīq* (*Jawhar*, 140).

And after this comes the permissible (*mubāḥ*).
The non-legislated [rulings] are of two types:

1. The unlawful (*ḥarām*)
2. The offensive (*makrūh*)

These two are followed by the 'nullifier (*mufsid*) of acts started'.

THE EIGHT TYPES OF LEGAL RULINGS: DEFINITIONS AND LEGAL CONSEQUENCES

Thus, in total, there are eight types [of legislated and non-legislated rulings which we will discuss below]:

1. [The Obligatory (*farḍ*)]

As for the obligatory act,[24] then this is what has been established by way of decisive proofs[25] (*dalīl qaṭʿī*) and is devoid of any ambiguity.[26]

24 When the *farḍ* is mentioned unqualified, it normally refers to the *farḍ qaṭʿī* or *farḍ ʿilmī*, which is what the author is defining.

25 That is, decisive in both its reliability (*thubūt*) and meaning or intended signification (*dalāla*). It is important to mention here, before delving into the various definitions, that proofs or evidences related to revelation are usually studied through the lens of reliability and meaning, each one assessed as either being decisive or indecisive therein:

1. Reliability (*thubūt*)
  a. Decisive in its reliability (*qaṭʿī al-thubūt*)
  b. Indecisive in its reliability (*ẓannī al-thubūt*)

2. Meaning (*dalāla*)
  a. Decisive in its meaning (*qaṭʿī al-dalāla*)
  b. Indecisive in its meaning (*ẓannī al-dalāla*)

Hence, based on the above categorisation there are only four types of proofs:

1. Decisive in both their reliability and their meaning, like certain verses of the Qur'an and *mutawātir* narrations
2. Decisive in their reliability, but indecisive in their meaning, like certain verses of the Qur'an that possess more than one meaning
3. Indecisive in their reliability, but decisive in their meaning, like solitary narrations (*āḥād*) whose meanings are definite
4. Indecisive in both their reliability and their meaning, like solitary narrations whose meanings are indefinite (*Radd*, 1:186; *al-Nahr al-Fā'iq*, 1:24)

26 Although the definition of the obligatory (*farḍ*) given by the author is com-

Its legal consequence is reward for performing it, punishment (*ʿiqāb*) for its non-performance[27] without an excuse,[28] and disbelief by disbelieving in that [of the obligatory] which is agreed upon.[29]

2. [The Necessary (*wājib*)]

The *wājib* is that which has been established by way of proofs that are uncertain.[30]

Its legal consequence is the same as that of an obligatory act with regards to [its] performance[31] but not with regards to belief, such that the one who

---

monly cited, it is considered by some to be 'loose', in that it fails to stop the inclusion of those things that are not considered obligatory, like a supererogatory act which has also been established by definite proofs and is devoid of any ambiguity, e.g. the verse in the Qur'an which states, '*when you have completed the rites of pilgrimage you may hunt*' (Q 5:2) – hunting here being merely permissible and not obligatory. That is why some scholars mention that a more clear and inclusive definition is to say that a *farḍ* is 'that which has been established by decisive proofs, and the one who neglects it totally without a valid excuse is deserving of punishment (*ʿiqāb*)' (*Minḥat al-Khāliq*, 1:24). However, in reality this objection can be answered by postulating that the actual intended meaning of the phrase 'devoid of any ambiguity' is that it is devoid of any ambiguity in both its reliability *and* meaning (i.e. it must signify obligation in both), or it can be said that the definition should be interpreted as 'that whose *obligation* has been established' (*Nasamāt al-Asḥār*, 164, emphasis added).

27 What is meant by punishment (*ʿiqāb*) is punishment with hellfire.

28 Examples of a valid excuse being coercion or having a legal dispensation due to an illness or being a traveller, in which case one is not considered sinful. It is important to note here that if it is left in disdain (*istikhfāf*), then it is not only sinful, but is tantamount to disbelief (*Jawhar*, 142; *Nūr al-Anwār*, 2:45).

29 Because it is not disbelief to deny the obligation of an obligatory act that is differed upon, which is known as the *farḍ ʿamalī* or *farḍ ẓannī* and is a degree lower than that of the *farḍ qaṭʿī*. However, similar to the *farḍ qaṭʿī*, neglecting the performance of a *farḍ ʿamalī* (like the *farḍ ʿilmī*) renders the act null, e.g. not wiping a quarter of the head in *wuḍū'* (*Jawhar*, 142).

30 That is, it is indecisive in either its reliability (*thubūt*) or intended meaning (*dalāla*).

31 That is, it must be performed; however, the non-performance of a *wājib* act does not nullify the act but rather it is rendered severely deficient, and therefore either its repetition or the performance of a 'repairing' act is required. For example, the recital of the Fātiḥa in prayer is a necessary component of prayer that if left unintentionally does not invalidate the prayer but necessitates that one performs the forgetfulness prostration or *sajdat al-sahw*. Similar to the *farḍ*, however, leaving a *wājib* act without a valid excuse is extremely sinful and deserving of punishment

denies it is not rendered a disbeliever.[32]

3. [The Sunna]

The sunna is what the Messenger of Allah ﷺ [or the rightly guided caliphs][33] performed regularly[34] but left once or twice.[35]

Its legal consequence is reward for performing it and rebuke (*'itāb*) for its non-performance.[36]

---

with hellfire (*al-Talwīḥ*, 2:259; *Radd*, 1:187).

32 Because of the lack of full certainty with which the act has been established. As long as something has not been established in a definite and certain manner, its denial alone cannot render one a disbeliever.

33 As the way of any of the rightly guided caliphs in the Ḥanafī school is also considered from the sunna as per the statement of the Messenger of Allah ﷺ, 'So hold fast upon my sunna and the sunna of the rightly guided caliphs' (*Abū Dāwūd*, 7:16.4607), and other such hadiths. Although, it is worth noting that in general, the sunna of the Messenger of Allah ﷺ is considered stronger (in legal terms) than that of his Companions (*Kashf al-Asrār*, 2:308; *Jawhar*, 144).

34 'Abd al-Ghanī al-Nābulsī postulates that the meaning of *muwādhaba* or performing regularly is that 'its performance is greater than its non-performance' (*Jawhar*, 144).

35 That is, it is left in this manner without a valid excuse; Ibn Nujaym states, 'in *al-Taḥrīr*, he adds that it [the definition of sunna] should include, "left sometimes without an excuse," to entail that it does not imply necessity' (*al-Baḥr*, 1:41). In general, 'a sunna is that which the Messenger of Allah ﷺ performed regularly. If it was never left, then it is evidence for its being an emphasised sunna. [However,] if it was left sometimes, then it is evidence for its being a non-emphasised sunna. And, if it was combined with rebuke for the one who does not perform it, then it is evidence for necessity' (*al-Baḥr*, 1:42).

36 More specifically, there are two types of sunnas and each one has a different consequence with regards to its performance or neglect:

1. The sunnas of guidance (*sunan al-hudā*) or the emphasised sunnas (*al-sunan al-mu'akkada*)

These sunnas are considered symbolic of the religion itself and leaving them persistently without an excuse entails wrongdoing (*iṣā'a*), rebuke (*'itāb*) and offense (*karāha*), since leaving them is considered from not taking the religion seriously. Denying a sunna of this type is not tantamount to disbelief but innovation (*bid'a*); although disbelief is feared for leaving such sunnas out of disdain (*istikhfāf*). The prayer in congregation, the *adhān* and the *iqāma* are some examples of this type of sunna.

2. The additional sunnas (*sunan al-zawā'id*) or the non-emphasised sunnas (*sunan ghayr mu'akkada*)

4. [The Recommended (*mustaḥabb*)]

The recommended is what the Messenger of Allah ﷺ performed sometimes but left at other times;[37] and [it also includes] that which the pious predecessors[38] deemed good.

Its legal consequence is reward for its performance and a lack of rebuke for its non-performance.

5. [The Permissible (*mubāḥ*)]

The permissible is that which the slave is given a choice between performing or not performing.

Its legal consequence is a lack of reward or punishment for [either] performing [it] or leaving [it].[39]

These are sunnas whose neglect does not necessitate wrongdoing or offense, as they are not symbolic of the religion itself and are not considered from those things that 'complete' the religion. The dress of the Messenger of Allah ﷺ, the way he stood, sat and ate are all examples of this type of sunna. A person is rewarded if he performs them but is not punished for neglecting them. In general, they are considered similar to the desirable act (*mustaḥabb*) (*Nūr al-Anwār*, 2:51–52; *Jawhar*, 143–145; *Radd*, 1:196).

37 That is, he ﷺ did not perform it regularly, leaving it more than he performed it. Or, he encouraged people to perform it, but did not perform it himself (*Jawhar*, 145; *al-Baḥr*, 1;69).

38 'Abd al-Ghanī al-Nābulsī states that 'the intended meaning of the pious predecessors (*salaf*) is our early Imams: Abū Ḥanīfa and his companions' (*Jawhar*, 145). Our esteemed teacher, Dr Ṣalāḥ Abūl-Ḥājj, comments upon this understanding by saying, 'The restriction of the meaning of [the term] *salaf* [to the Imams of the Ḥanafī school] by Shaykh 'Abd al-Ghanī is brilliant, and which many people are ignorant of. This is because the *salaf* are manifold and they have [separate] schools of law in understanding legal rulings. And so, it is incumbent that when one says, "I am a follower of the *salaf*," to define which school [one means] from their [multiple] schools, such as the school of Kufa, which is what the Ḥanafī school relies upon for its understanding ... If one does not define [what one means by the "*salaf*"], then one will become severely astray, because the understandings of the *salaf* differ and many opinions have been related from them on every issue, and it is well known that the application of multiple opinions to one issue at the same time is impossible' (*al-Mirqāt*, 153–154).

39 However, it is important to note that a permissible action can become an act of devotion by making a pious intention and hence deserving of reward, e.g. eating food to gain strength to worship Allah or to sleep in the day so that one can wake up for the night vigil prayer. In the same manner, it can also become sinful and deserving of punishment if therein is an evil intention, e.g. wearing

6. [The Unlawful (*muḥarram*)][40]

The unlawful is that whose prohibition has been established without any contradiction to it.[41]

Its legal consequence is reward for leaving [it] for the sake of Allah Almighty,[42] punishment (*'iqāb*) for performing [it],[43] and disbelief by considering that which is agreed upon[44] [as being unlawful] to be lawful.

7. [The Offensive (*makrūh*)]

As for the offensive, then this is whose prohibition has been established with [some] contradiction [to it].[45]

---

luxurious clothes as a way to boast and brag over others (*al-Ta'līqa al-Tihāmiyya*, 25; *al-Durar al-Mubāḥa*, 9).

40 When the unlawful is mentioned unconditionally, it normally refers to the *ḥarām qaṭ'ī* or *ḥarām 'ilmī*. It is similar in strength to the *farḍ 'ilmī* because both are established by decisive evidences. Eating carrion, drinking alcohol, fornication and backbiting are all examples of decisively unlawful acts.

41 That is, without the presence of any contradicting evidence to its prohibition that indicates its lawfulness (*al-Mirqāt*, 153).

42 That is, one had the ability to perform it but did not. Otherwise, one is not rewarded for leaving it, like the impotent man leaving fornication (*Jawhar*, 147).

43 That is, without a valid excuse.

44 Because it is not disbelief to deny the obligation of an unlawful act that is differed upon. This is what is known as the *ḥarām 'amalī* or *ḥarām ẓannī*, which is a degree lower than that of the *ḥarām qaṭ'ī*. It is, however, similar to the *ḥarām qaṭ'ī* in that one must abstain from it, and the one who fails to do so is deserving of punishment in hellfire.

45 That is, there is evidence for its impermissibility but also for its permissibility, and thus the basis of its offensiveness is indecisive proofs. Depending on the strength of evidence for its impermissibility, the *makrūh* can be categorised into two well-known types:

1. The severely offensive (*makrūh taḥrīm*)
This is an offensive act which is closer to the unlawful than the lawful and is of two types:

a. That which is the result of neglecting a *wājib* (*karāhat ithm*)
To abstain from this type of offensive act is *wājib* and it is established in the same way as the *wājib*. The one who fails to abstain from this type of offense is deserving of sin (*ithm*) and of being punished with hellfire (*'iqāb*). One is rewarded for abstaining from such an act, but the reward is less than the reward of abstaining from an unlawful act.

Its legal consequence is reward[46] for leaving it in the manner described,[47] the fear of punishment for performing [it], and not [falling into] disbelief for regarding it as lawful.

8. [The Nullifier (*mufsid*)]

As for the nullifier, then this is that which invalidates an act already begun.

Its legal consequence is punishment (*'iqāb*) for doing it intentionally[48] and its lack of [if done] unintentionally.

Subsequently, know that the prayer comprises the first four [categories][49] legally[50] and the other four may be present by way of human nature.[51] Therefore, it is incumbent to describe each category in detail and to enumerate them in a comprehensive but brief manner, arranging them in eight chapters to make it easy for the believers.

---

b. That which is the result of neglecting an emphasised sunna (*karāhat iṣā'a*)
Leaving an emphasised sunna or a sunna of guidance is considered severely offensive. The punishment for the one who persistently performs this type of offense is the same as neglecting an emphasised sunna, and it is also established in the same way as the emphasised sunna.

2. Slightly offensive (*makrūh tanzīh*)
This is an offensive act which is closer to the lawful than the unlawful and is equivalent to the non-emphasised sunna. The one who performs it is *not* deserving of punishment; however, if he does abstain from it, then he is given a small reward. The non-performance of a non-emphasised sunna is considered slightly offensive (*Ḥāshiyat al-Ṭaḥṭāwī*, 1:123; *al-Baḥr*, 2:60; *Jawhar*, 147; *Radd*, 9:409–410; *al-Talwīḥ*, 2:264).

46 But reward that is slightly less than that of leaving an unlawful act (*Jawhar*, 147).

47 That is, leaving it for the sake of Allah similar to the unlawful (*Jawhar*, 147).

48 Allah says, '*do not let your deeds go to waste*' (Q 47:33).

49 That is, the obligatory, necessary, sunna and recommended.

50 That is, these four categories have been mandated in prayer by way of Sacred Law.

51 That is, they are not mandated through Sacred Law; however, one performs them because man is naturally disposed to making mistakes, forgetfulness and laziness (*Jawhar*, 149).

CHAPTER 1

The Obligatory (*Farā'iḍ*)

They [the obligatory acts] are fifteen; some are external[52] [to the prayer] whilst some are internal.[53] As for the external, they are eight:

1. Time[54]
2. Purity of the body[55]

52 These are what are known as the preconditions or *shurūṭ*; they are not performed within the actual prayer but have to be fulfilled before the prayer for it to be valid.

53 These are the actual components or *arkān* within the prayer that must be performed; otherwise, the prayer is deemed invalid.

54 Each of the five prayers has a specific time period in which it must be prayed:

Fajr: It begins with a light spreading horizontally across the horizon, also known as the true dawn (*al-fajr al-ṣādiq*), and ends with the rising of the sun.
Ẓuhr: It begins with the declension of the sun from the zenith (*zawāl*) until the shadow of a thing reaches double its size (excluding the zenith shadow).
'Aṣr: It begins with the expiring of *ẓuhr* and ends when the sun sets.
Maghrib: It begins when the sun sets and ends with the setting of the white twilight (*al-shafaq al-abyaḍ*).
'Ishā' and *witr*: They begin when the white twilight disappears and ends with the appearance of the true dawn (*al-fajr al-ṣādiq*). Although both *'ishā'* and *witr* have the same time period, *witr* is not prayed before the *'ishā'* prayer such that if it were done so deliberately, then it would be considered invalid (*Tuḥfa*, 60–61; *Hadiyyat al-Ṣa'lūk*, 43).

It is crucial to note here that before engaging in prayer one must have conviction that the time has entered for that prayer to be valid; mere conjecture is not sufficient.

55 Allah says, '*Cleanse yourself* (Q 74:4). There are two types of impurities that concern the body:

3. [Purity of] clothing[56]

4. [Purity of] place[57]

---

1. Ritual impurities (*al-najāsa al-ḥukmiyya*)
They can be further classified into two categories:

a. Minor ritual impurity (*al-ḥadath al-aṣghar*)
One enters this state by doing anything that necessitates *wuḍū'* such as passing wind, urinating or passing stool.

b. Major ritual impurity (*al-ḥadath al-akbar*)
One enters this state by doing anything that necessitates *ghusl* such as sexual intercourse, ejaculation or menstruation.

2. Real impurities (*al-najāsa al-ḥaqīqiyya*)
They are actual physical impurities that are legally considered filthy such as human excrement or urine. They are of two types:

a. Moderate impurity (*al-najāsa al-mukhaffafa*)
For example, the urine of animals whose meat is lawful to consume. If this type of impurity is on one's body, then if it covers less than a quarter of the body, it is excused. However, if it covers more than a quarter of the body, then the prayer will not be valid.

b. Severe impurity (*al-najāsa al-ghalīdha*)
For example, alcohol, blood, urine or faeces. The weight of one dirham (approximately 5 g) of a solid impurity of this type, and the amount that equates to the surface area of the palm of one's hand when extended (approximately 3–5 cm) of a liquid impurity of this type, is excused (*Jawhar*, 154; *al-Ikhtiyār*, 1:110–111).

It is important to note here that for both the moderate and severe impurities, if they are scattered around the body, then they must be combined together and if they exceed the excused amount, then it is no longer excused.

56 Clothing, in legal terms, is defined as that which is on a person that moves if the person moves in prayer, e.g. a shirt or a hat. This, however, would exclude, for example, a long tail of a garment which stayed static even if the person bowed or prostrated. Impurities on clothing follow the same rulings as a real impurity found on the body. One should note, however, that any impurity on one's clothing is *not* combined with any impurity on the body – each is considered separately (*Marāqī*, 2:93–94).

57 For the validity of the prayer the minimum obligation is that the ground the feet are standing on and the place where the forehead rests when prostrating are pure. The purity of the place where one places the hands and knees when prostrating is sunna; that is, the prayer will still be valid as long as the impurity does not transfer and adhere to the person praying, in which case, one is considered to be carrying the impurity. With regards to the nose, 'Abd al-Ghanī al-Nābulsī states that it is not necessary for the place where the nose is placed to be pure, because the part of the nose which is placed on the ground is too small for a severe impurity the

5. Covering the private area (*satr al-ʿawra*)[58]

6. Facing the *qibla*[59]

7. The intention[60]

---

amount of one dirham to cover (*Jawhar*, 164; *al-Mabsūṭ*, 1:205).

58 Males must cover the area below the navel up to and including the knees. Females, however, are obliged to cover their whole body including the hair, with the exception of the face, hands and feet, when in prayer; when outside of prayer, the feet must also be covered according to the more correct opinion. The *ʿawra* must be covered with something that does not reveal what is underneath, and so it cannot be too thin. It should be noted that if the feet *are* uncovered, then one should make sure not to uncover the ankles when bowing or prostrating. The area is considered uncovered if a quarter of any given limb (e.g. a quarter of the shin, the thigh or the abdomen) is exposed, and stays exposed for the length of a whole integral (*rukn*) of prayer, which is normally calculated as the length it would take to say '*Subḥāna Llāh*' thrice. If little areas are exposed throughout the body, then they are combined; if they accumulate to a quarter of the smallest limb exposed, then the prayer is also considered invalid (*Minḥa*, 119; *Marāqī*, 2:98, 102–103; *Jawhar*, 164; *Radd*, 2:74-75).

59 There are four rulings with regards to facing the *qibla* depending on one's location:

1. The one who can see the Kaʿba
This person must face the actual Kaʿba. This means that if an arrow were to fly level at the centre of his forehead, it would hit the actual Kaʿba or the equivalent space above it.

2. The one who cannot see the Kaʿba (including the Meccan)
This person must face the actual Kaʿba (like the one who can see the Kaʿba) or face its direction, which means that one is not totally in the wrong direction but a part of one's forehead is still facing the Kaʿba. This is generally calculated as 45 degrees to the left and right of the actual direction of the *qibla*.

3. The one in fear (*khā'if*)
His *qibla* is the direction of his enemy or the thing he fears.

4. The one who does not know the direction of the *qibla* and is taking a calculated estimate (*mutaḥarrī*)
His *qibla* is whichever way his calculation directs him. This means that if he prays in any other direction and it became clear after completing the prayer that that direction was in fact the direction of the Kaʿba, then his prayer is considered invalid (*Jawhar*, 165; *Marāqī*, 2:62–63; *al-Mirqāt*, 160).

60 That is, to intend the prayer in one's heart; verbalising it is not obligatory but recommended. It is also recommended that the intention is coupled with the actual *takbīr*; however, delaying the *takbīr* after the intention is permissible as long as one does not perform anything between the intention and actual prayer that is

8. The opening *takbīr*[61]

As for the internal, then they are seven:

1. Standing (*qiyām*)[62]
2. Recitation (*qirā'a*)[63]

---

not related to the prayer, e.g. buying or selling, talking, eating or drinking. If the intention is interrupted by actions that are related to the prayer, like performing *wuḍū'* or walking to the congregational prayer, then the intention is still valid. When making the intention one must intend a specific prayer if one is performing a *farḍ*, make-up (*qaḍā'*) or *wājib* prayer. It is also permissible instead to intend to pray the prescribed prayer of the time for all obligatory prayers except the Friday prayer. With make-up prayers, if one can remember which prayer exactly one is making up, then this is better. Otherwise, if there are too many prayers, from a long time ago, then one can make the intention 'to pray the first missed prayer from all the missed prayers upon me'. It is not obligatory with sunna and supererogatory prayers to specify which sunna it is, e.g. one does not need to say one is praying the four sunnas before *ẓuhr* or the two sunnas before *fajr*, rather the mere intention to pray a sunna prayer is sufficient.
It is also important to mention here that intending the number of units is likewise not obligatory, and therefore even if one intended to pray five units of *ẓuhr* but then prayed four, then one's *ẓuhr* is still valid. If one is praying in congregation, then one would also need to make the intention of following the imam (*Minḥa*, 121–122; *Marāqī*, 2:70–72).

61 According to Abū Ḥanīfa, the minimal obligation (*farḍ*) required to enter into prayer is to utter any sincere word of remembrance (*dhikr khāliṣ*) like the statements '*Allāh jalīl*' or '*Allāh ʿaẓīm*'. However, it is necessary (*wājib*) to utter a form that stems from the Arabic root *k-b-r*, like '*Allāh kabīr*' or '*Allāh akbar*' (as will be mentioned in Chapter 2). It is vital to note that one of the preconditions of its validity is to utter it whilst in a standing position. With regards to someone who lacks the ability to speak and cannot verbalise the *takbīr*, then the mere intention to begin the prayer is sufficient (*Marāqī*, 2:66–67).

62 The one who has the capacity to stand *and* the capacity to prostrate must stand during the recitation when praying a *farḍ* or *wājib* prayer. In the instance where one is capable of standing but not prostrating, then it is better to sit and pray. One is considered standing if after extending the arms they do not reach the knees; this is, of course, the minimal obligation (*Marāqī*, 2:75; *Tuḥfa*, 114).

63 The minimal obligation (*farḍ*), according to Abū Ḥanīfa, is to recite at least one verse, even if it is short composing only of two words, in any two units of the *farḍ* prayer and each single unit of the *witr* prayer and supererogatory prayer. According to the *ṣāḥibayn*, however, the minimal obligation is to recite three short verses or one long verse. The shortest verse in the Qur'an comprising six letters is '*thumma naẓara*' (Q 74:21), and thus any verse which is eighteen letters or more,

3. Bowing (*rukūʿ*)[64]
4. Prostration (*sujūd*)[65]
5. The last sitting (*al-qaʿda al-akhīra*)[66]
6. Sequence (*tartīb*), in those things that are legislated to be performed either once in each unit or [once in] the whole prayer[67]
7. To exit [the prayer] with an act performed by the person praying[68]

---

is considered one long verse. With regards to the one who is incapable of reciting, like the dumb or illiterate, he can simply stand silently (*Jawhar*, 168).

64 The minimal obligation is if one were to extend the arms, they would reach the knees.

65 The minimal obligation is to place some of the forehead on the ground. It is important to note that some scholars also held placing the nose on the ground to be an obligation, even though its being *wājib* is generally considered the stronger opinion. Likewise, there is also discussion with regards to the feet; according to Kāshgharī and others at least one toe of one foot must touch the ground for the validity of the prostration, whereas others felt that at least one toe from both feet must touch the ground for its validity. Although the sounder opinion is that this is a sunna, one must be careful not to neglect it when prostrating as there is a strong difference of opinion in the school (*Munya* and *Ḥalabī Kabīr*, 284–285; *Durr* and *Radd*, 2:180; *al-Mirqāt*, 163–164).

66 The minimal obligation is to sit, in any position, for the length it takes to recite the *tashahhud*, *after* having performed all the other components of prayer (*Marāqī*, 2:87–88).

67 For example, standing, bowing and prostrating are all sanctioned to be performed once in one unit, and the last sitting is something that is performed only once in the whole prayer, and therefore these acts must be performed in order or sequence. This means, the standing must precede the bowing, and the bowing must precede the prostration, and the last sitting must be preceded with all the other integrals of prayer, otherwise the component is deemed invalid and consequently the prayer likewise. For example, if one bowed after prostrating, then the prostration is invalid, and one must prostrate again after bowing. With regards to actions that are repeated more than once in one unit, like both prostrations, then the sequence between them is *wājib*. Hence, one could theoretically perform one prostration in one unit and three in the next, and the prayer would still be valid, but severely deficient (*Jawhar*, 179; *Radd*, 2:135).

68 According to Abū Ḥanīfa (as per the understanding of Imam al-Bardaʿī), it is obligatory (*farḍ*) to intentionally exit the prayer by performing an act that takes one out of the prayer when one has finished praying, regardless of whether the act is considered an act of worship, like giving the *salāms*, or is actually sinful (i.e. to exit the prayer in this manner is considered sinful), like drinking or eating. However, it is not a *farḍ* according to the *ṣāḥibayn*, and there are some scholars – like

Karkhī – who felt that this was not an obligation even according to Abū Ḥanīfa. This latter opinion is generally considered the stronger and sounder opinion, because ultimately its obligation has been extrapolated from indecisive evidences (which generally do not imply obligation (*faraḍiyya*)). The consequence of considering it a *farḍ* is that if after sitting the length of the *tashahhud* in the last sitting one nullified the *wuḍū'*, the prayer would be considered incomplete and one would need to either restart the prayer or perform *wuḍū'* and return to the prayer, and then exit the prayer by performing a relevant act. Whereas, according to the other opinion, the prayer would be valid but severely deficient (*Jawhar*, 169; *Fatḥ Bāb al-'Ināya*, 1:230; *al-Baḥr*, 1:568–569).

CHAPTER 2

The Necessary (*Wājibāt*)[69]

They [the necessary acts] are twenty-one. Some concern all [types of] persons praying[70] and all [types of] prayers;[71] and these are seven. Whilst others are specific and only concern some persons and some prayers; and these are fourteen.

As for the generic,[72] [they are:]

1. The words of '*al-takbīr*' for the [opening] prohibitive *takbīr*[73]
2. The first sitting (*al-qa'dat al-ūlā*)
3. The [recitation of the] *tashahhud* in both sittings[74]

69 Before delving into the *wājib* actions of prayer, it is important to mention that if any *wājib* action is neglected, the prayer remains valid; however, it becomes severely deficient and will need to be 'repaired'. The act needed to 'repair' the prayer will depend on whether the *wājib* was missed deliberately or by mistake. If done by mistake or forgetfully, then it will necessitate the forgetfulness prostration. However, if it was done deliberately, then one is considered sinful and it in turn becomes *wājib* to repeat the prayer in the time period of the prescribed prayer. After the prayer time, it is recommended to repeat the prayer, but not *wājib* (*Jawhar*, 180).

70 That is, either the imam, someone who is in congregation with the imam or the one praying alone.

71 That is, regardless of whether the prayer is *farḍ*, *wājib*, sunna or supererogatory.

72 That is, they apply to all persons and all prayers.

73 This is to begin the prayer with a form that contains the Arabic root letters *k-b-r*, e.g. '*Allāh akbar*', '*Allāh al-akbar*', '*Allāh kabīr*' or '*Allāh al-kibār*', with it being from the sunna to choose the phrase '*Allāh akbar*' from amongst them (*Jawhar*, 166).

74 On the authority of Ibn Mas'ūd who said, 'We would say whilst in prayer behind the Messenger of Allah ﷺ, "Peace be upon Allah, peace be upon so-and-so," and so the Messenger of Allah ﷺ said to us one day, "Verily Allah, He is peace,

4. Having composure when bowing and prostrating[75]
5. To perform each *farḍ* in its [prescribed] place[76]
6. And each *wājib* likewise[77]
7. To exit [the prayer] with the words '*al-salām*'[78]

As for the specific, they are:

---

and so if one of you sits in prayer, then let him say, '*At-taḥiyyātu li-Llāhi wa-ṣ-ṣalawātu wa-ṭ-ṭayyibāt(u), as-salāmu 'alayka ayyuha n-nabiyyu wa-raḥmatu Llāhi wa-barakātuh(u), as-salāmu 'alaynā wa-'alā 'ibādi Llāhi ṣ-ṣāliḥīn, ashhadu an lā ilāha illā Llāhu wa-ashhadu anna Muḥammadan 'abduhu wa-rasūluh(u)*''" (*Bukhārī*, 1:166.831).

This is what is known as the *tashahhud* of Ibn Mas'ūd and it is *wājib* to utter these exact words, no more and no less, and in the same word order in *both* sittings (*Jawhar*, 171). Tirmidhī narrates in his *Sunan*, 'From Khuṣayf who said, "I saw the Prophet ﷺ in my sleep and I said, 'Messenger of Allah! The people are differing over [the wording of] the *tashahhud*!' He ﷺ replied, 'Stick to Ibn Mas'ūd's *tashahhud*'"' (*Tirmidhī*, 2:82).

75 That is, to keep the limbs motionless for at least the length it would take one to say '*Subḥāna Llāh*'. This ruling is specific to the bowing and prostrating. As for having composure between prostrations and in the standing after bowing, then this is sunna. Abū Yūsuf, however, considered composure when bowing and prostrating *farḍ* and thus one should make sure not to neglect it (*Jawhar*, 173).

76 That is, to perform each obligation in the specific place it has been sanctioned in *without* any delay. For example, if after finishing the recitation one continued standing, without reciting the Qur'an or any form of remembrance, for the length it would take one to say '*Subḥāna Llāh*' thrice, then one must perform the forgetfulness prostration for delaying the bowing (the next component). Likewise, this includes repeating actions, e.g. bowing twice, performing a third prostration, sitting in the first unit or any similar act that comes between two obligatory acts. 'Performing each obligation in its proper place' could also signify – as mentioned in Chapter 1 – keeping the sequence between actions that are repeated *more* than once in one unit like the two prostrations (*Durr*, 2:144; *Jawhar*, 173).

77 That is, the *wājib* acts of prayer, similar to the obligatory actions, must be performed without any delay in their proper place, e.g. reciting a sura immediately after completing the recitation of the Fātiḥa.

78 That is, it is *wājib* to exit the prayer by saying '*al-salām*' twice. To add the words ''*alaykum wa-raḥmat Allāh*' is sunna. With the utterance of the first '*salām*' one exits the prayer, and so if a man joined the congregation after the imam had uttered the words '*salām*', but before he had said ''*alaykum wa-raḥmat Allāh*', then he has not joined the congregation as the imam has already exited the prayer (*Durr* and *Radd*, 2:143; *Marāqī*, 2:114).

1. To specify the first two units for the recitation [of the Qur'an][79]
2. And to [also] specify the [recitation of the] Fātiḥa in them[80]
3. To limit its recitation [i.e. that of the Fātiḥa] to once only[81]
4. To join a sura, three short verses or one long verse to it [the Fātiḥa][82]
5. To precede it [the sura] with the Fātiḥa[83]

These [last five] are for those who must recite [in prayer]:84

6. The [recital of the] *qunūt* in [the] *witr* [prayer][85]

---

79 That is, when praying a three- or four-unit obligatory prayer it is *wājib* to recite the Qur'an in the first two units. It is reported that 'Alī and Ibn Mas'ūd both said, 'Recite in the first two [units] and glorify in the other two' (*Muṣannaf Ibn Abī Shayba*, 1:326.3732; *Jawhar*, 174).

80 That is, to only recite the Fātiḥa in the first two units of an obligatory prayer. As for a *wājib*, sunna or supererogatory prayer then it is *wājib* to recite the Fātiḥa in all of their units (*Jawhar*, 174).

81 That is, it is *wājib* to not repeat the recital of the Fātiḥa straight after reciting the first Fātiḥa before the recital of the sura in the first two units of a *farḍ* or *wājib* prayer. Repeating it in this manner necessitates the forgetfulness prostration; however, repeating it after having already read a sura does not. Repeating it forgetfully in the third or fourth unit does not necessitate the forgetfulness prostration (*Jawhar*, 174; *Radd*, 2:135).

82 That is, it is *wājib* to do this immediately after reciting the Fātiḥa in the first two units of a *farḍ* prayer, and in every unit of a *wājib*, sunna or supererogatory prayer.

83 If one recited a sura (or anything with which the minimal obligation of recitation is fulfilled) before the Fātiḥa, then one should repeat the Fātiḥa, recite the sura again after it and then perform the forgetfulness prostration at the end of the prayer (*Radd*, 2:135).

84 That is, these five only apply to the imam, the one praying alone and the latecomer. They do not apply to the one praying in congregation with the imam as he does not recite in prayer (*Jawhar*, 174).

85 The lexical significance of the word '*qunūt*' in Arabic is obedience, supplication and standing (i.e. in devotion to Allah); Allah says, '*and stand before Allah in devotion (qānitīn)*' (Q 2:238). In the prayer, it signifies an unadulterated supplication of that which cannot be asked from other than Allah. The *qunūt* is recited silently in the third unit of the *witr* prayer after the recital of the sura but before the bowing. Of the supplications that are considered sunna to recite by the scholars of the school is the following: '*Allāh-humma innā nasta'īnuka wa-nastaghfiruka wa-natūbu ilayk(a), nu'minu bi-ka wa-natawakkalu 'alayk(a), wa-nuthnī 'alayka l-khayr(a), nashkuruka wa-lā nakfuruk(a), wa-nakhla'u wa-natruku man yafjurak(a), Allāh-humma iyyāka na'budu wa-laka nuṣallī wa-nasjud(u), wa-ilayka*

7. To recite loudly, in its proper place, when praying in congregation[86]
8. And reciting silently [in the proper places] likewise[87]
9. To stay silent when praying behind the imam when the imam is reciting[88]
10. To follow the imam in any state one finds him in, even if that would not be considered from his prayer[89]
11. [To perform] the prostration of recital [in prayer] for [both] the imam[90] and the one praying alone
12. [To perform] the *takbīrs* of the Eid prayer[91]
13. And the *takbīr* for the bowing in them[92]
14. [To perform] the prostration of forgetfulness[93] for [both] the

---

nas'ā wa-naḥfid(u), narjū raḥmataka wa-nakhshā 'adhābak(a), inna 'adhābaka l-jidda bi-l-kuffāri mulḥiq' (*Jawhar*, 185–186; *Muṣannaf Ibn Abī Shayba*, 2:95.6893; *Marāqī*, 2:298–302). If one is not able to recite the above supplication, then one can supplicate with '*Allāh-humma ghfirlī*' thrice, or '*Rabbanā ātinā fī d-dunyā ḥasana(tan), wa-fī l-ākhirati ḥasana(tan), wa-qinā 'adhāba n-nār*', or '*Yā Rabb*' thrice. It is important to mention here that if one is praying the *witr* in congregation (in Ramadan), then both the imam and the follower recite the *qunūt* supplication silently (*Marāqī*, 2:302–307).

86 That is, in the two units of *fajr*, the first two units of *maghrib*, the first two units of *'ishā'*, the Friday prayer, the Eid prayer and the *tarawīḥ* and *witr* prayers in Ramadan (*Radd*, 2:144).

87 That is, in the *ẓuhr*, *'aṣr*, third unit of *maghrib*, last two units of *'ishā'* and any supererogatory prayers performed in the morning, and the *khusūf* and *istisqā'* prayers (*Radd*, 2:144).

88 That is, regardless of whether the imam was reciting loudly or silently. Reciting behind the imam is severely offensive, but it does not invalidate the prayer (*Radd*, 2:145).

89 'Abd al-Ghanī al-Nābulsī states, 'If the follower joins the prayer with the imam and the imam was in the standing position after the bowing, or in prostration, then it is *wājib* for him to follow him in that. If he does not, then he is sinful, but his following will still be valid' (*Jawhar*, 178).

90 This also includes the one following the imam.

91 That is, the six extra *takbīrs* of the Eid prayer (three in each unit) are *wājib*.

92 That is, the *takbīr* for the bowing in the second unit of both Eid prayers (*Tabyīn*, 1:194).

93 These are two prostrations performed straight after the *tashahhud* in the final sitting. They are performed by giving the *salāms* once to the right side only after the *tashahhud* and then prostrating twice. After performing these extra two

imam and the one praying alone for leaving a necessary act from the initial eight[94] of the second category,[95] and for [leaving] all of them from the first category,[96] with the exception of '[having] composure [when bowing and prostrating]'[97] as it is not necessary in and of itself[98]

prostrations, one should repeat the *tashahhud*, send salutations and supplicate as normal (*Marāqī*, 1:442).

94 And therefore, this excludes numbers 10 to 14 from the 'specific' necessary acts. However, neglecting the *takbīr*s of Eid does in fact necessitate the prostration of forgetfulness (*Marāqī*, 2:116).

95 That is, the first eight from the 'specific' necessary acts.

96 That is, the 'generic' necessary acts.

97 The more correct opinion is that leaving composure forgetfully *does* in fact necessitate the prostration of forgetfulness (*al-Mirqāt*, 172).

98 That is, it is only considered necessary because it is a thing that 'completes' the bowing and prostration and is not a necessity in and of itself.

CHAPTER 3

The Sunna (*Sunan*)

They [the sunna acts] are twenty-seven.

The generic of them are seventeen, and they are:

1. To raise the hands when performing the opening *takbīr*[99]
2. And [to raise the hands] for the *qunūt*[100]
3. And [to raise the hands] for the *takbīrs* of the two Eid prayers
4. And extending the fingers therein[101]
5. The praise (*thanā'*)[102]

---

99 It is sunna for men to raise the hands until the thumbs are adjacent to the earlobes, and for women to raise them up to the chest as this is less revealing of their modesty. One can either raise them first and then proclaim the *takbīr* – which was the opinion of Abū Ḥanīfa and Muḥammad and what the majority of scholars are agreed upon – or raise them whilst proclaiming the *takbīr*, which has been related from Abū Yūsuf and preferred by certain scholars in the school (*Jawhar*, 183; *al-Mirqāt*, 173; *Fatḥ*, 1:283).

100 That is, to raise them when performing the *qunūt* supplication in the same manner described above.

101 That is, the fingers should not be clenched but kept open in a natural manner. It does not mean to widen the space between the fingers (*Jawhar*, 184).

102 The praise or *thanā'* is recited straight after the opening *takbīr* in an inaudible manner. The following is what should be recited as mentioned in certain narrations: '*Subḥānaka Llāh-humma wa-bi-ḥamdika wa-tabāraka smuka wa-taʿālā jadduka wa-lā ilāha ghayruk(a)*' (*Tirmidhī*, 2:9.242). One should not add anything to this formula in an obligatory prayer (*Jawhar*, 184).

6. To place the right [hand] over the left [hand][103]
7. [To perform] the *takbīr*s of moving [from one component of the prayer to another], including the [*takbīr* of the] *qunūt*
8. [Reciting] the glorifications of the bowing thrice[104]
9. To grasp the knees when bowing
10. And to space out the fingers therein[105]
11. To stand after bowing (*qawma*)
12. To sit between the prostrations
13. To prostrate on [all] seven limbs[106]
14. [Reciting] the glorifications of the prostration thrice[107]
15. To send salutations upon the Messenger ﷺ after the final *tashahhud*[108]

---

103 With regards to men, the right palm is placed on top of the left hand under the navel, whilst making a ring with the thumb and little finger around the left wrist. Women should place their hands on the chest without forming a ring around the wrist as this is considered less revealing (*Jawhar*, 184; *Marāqī*, 2:125).

104 That is, to say '*Subḥāna Rabbiya l-'aẓīm*' (Transcendent is my Lord the most Exalted) thrice. This is considered the least amount in establishing the sunna; to say it more than three times, in an odd amount, is considered better. However, the imam should not increase upon three times to make sure the prayer does not become wearisome upon the followers (*Jawhar*, 185).

105 One should grasp the knees with the hands and space out the fingers, straighten the back and legs and keep the head level with one's posterior. This is the only place where spacing the fingers is sanctioned to allow one to be able to straighten the back. Women, however, are excluded from this and should not space out their fingers or straighten the back as their prayer is based upon concealment (*Jawhar*, 185–186; *al-Mirqāt*, 178).

106 That is, the hands, knees, feet and head. On the authority of Ibn 'Abbās who said, 'The Messenger of Allah ﷺ said, "I have been ordered to prostrate upon seven limbs: on the forehead (and then pointed to his nose with his hand), the hands, the knees and the toes"' (*Bukhārī*, 1:163.812). Muṣṭafā Dīb al-Bughā comments upon the pointing of the nose by saying, 'That is, to indicate that the nose and the forehead are considered one limb' (*Bukhārī*, ed. Bughā, 1:280).

107 The formula one should use when glorifying is, '*Subḥāna Rabbiya l-a'lā*'. (Transcendent is my Lord the most Sublime). The rules mentioned above regarding the glorifications when bowing also apply here.

108 That is, the *tashahhud* in the last sitting. The formula one should use is the *Ṣalāt al-Ibrāhīmiyya*, which is as follows: '*Allāh-humma ṣalli 'alā Muḥammadin*

16. And to supplicate to Allah after it,[109] for oneself and all the believers[110]

17. To give *salāms* to the right and left[111]

The specific are ten:

1. For the Imam to recite the *takbīrāt* loudly[112]

2. For the follower to simultaneously [perform his opening *takbīr*] with the Imams [opening] *takbīr*[113]

3. To follow him in all of his actions[114]

---

wa-'alā ālī Muḥammadin kamā ṣallayta 'alā Ibrāhīma wa-'alā ālī Ibrāhīm(a), innaka ḥamīdun majīd. Allāh-humma bārik 'alā Muḥammadin wa-'alā ālī Muḥammadin kamā bārakta 'alā Ibrāhīma wa-'alā ālī Ibrāhīm(a), innaka ḥamīdun majīd' (*Bukhārī*, 4:146.3370). It should be noted that there is no harm in adding the term '*sayyidunā*' (our master) before the names of the Messenger of Allah ﷺ and the prophet Ibrāhīm ﷺ.

109 That is, after the *tashahhud*.

110 One must supplicate with a formula that has either been related from the Qur'an and Sunna or ask for something which can only be granted by Allah and *cannot* be granted by people. It is related from 'Ā'isha, 'that the Messenger of Allah ﷺ would supplicate in his prayer with, "*Allāh-humma innī a'ūdhu bi-ka min 'adhābi l-qabr, wa-a'ūdhu bi-ka min fitnati l-masīḥ d-dajjāl, wa-a'ūdhu bi-ka min fitnati l-maḥyā wa-fitnati l-mamāt. Allāh-humma innī a'ūdhu bi-ka mina l-ma'thami wa-l-maghram*"' (*Bukhārī*, 1:166.832).

It is important that in an obligatory or *wājib* prayer the supplication is only sanctioned after the *tashahhud* in the final sitting. This means that supplicating in the prostration, when bowing or in any other place in the prayer is considered offensive as it is to act in contrary to the sunna. There is, however, more leeway in supererogatory prayers and supplications are allowed in other than the last sitting.

111 That is, to turn the head first to the right side and then to the left when giving the *salāms*; it has been related from 'Āmir b. Sa'd from his father that he said, 'I would see the Messenger of Allah ﷺ turn his head right and left when giving the *salāms* until I was able to see the whiteness of his cheeks' (*Muslim*, 1:409.582).

112 That is, loud enough that the followers near him can hear it.

113 This is according to Abū Ḥanīfa, with the condition that the follower does not complete saying '*Allāh*' or '*akbar*' before the imam. Based upon this, if the follower completes saying '*Allāh*' with the imam or after him and completes saying '*akbar*' before the imam, then he has not entered the prayer. According to the *ṣāḥibayn*, however, the follower should perform his opening *takbīr* after the imam has done it, such that the follower says the first letter of the *takbīr* when the imam is on the last letter of his *takbīr* (*Jawhar*, 188; *Marāqī* and *Minnat al-Fattāḥ*, 2:122).

114 That is, to follow the imam simultaneously in all his movements without

4. To seek refuge (*taʿawwudh*)[115]
5. And lowering the voice therein[116]
6. And to mention the name of Allah (*tasmiya*) after it[117]
7. And lowering the voice therein

These [last] four are for the imam and the one praying alone.

8. For both of them to say '*Āmīn*' silently,[118] and [likewise] the follower in a loud prayer[119]
9. The [recital of the] *tasmīʿ*[120] for the imam[121] and the [recital of the] *taḥmīd*[122] for the one following [him]; the one praying alone should combine [between the two] in any prayer[123]
10. For men to lay out their left foot to sit on and raise the right [foot]

---

any delay.

115 That is, for the imam, the one praying alone or latecomer to recite '*Aʿūdhu bi-Llāhi mina sh-shayṭāni r-rajīm*' after reciting the praise (*thanā'*), once in the first unit before commencing the recitation. The follower does not recite it because he does not recite Qur'an in his prayer (*Marāqī*, 2:126).

116 That is, to seek refuge silently, but making sure that it is audible to oneself (*Jawhar*, 89).

117 That is, to say '*Bismi Llāhi r-raḥmāni r-raḥīm*' silently after seeking refuge (*taʿawwudh*) in the first unit, and at the start of every other unit before the recitation of the Fātiḥa (*Marāqī*, 2:126).

118 That is, for both the imam and the follower to say '*Āmīn*' at the end of the Fātiḥa silently.

119 That is, the follower in a loud prayer should say '*Āmīn*' silently. However, in a silent prayer there is no '*Āmīn*' for the follower, even if he hears the imam say '*wa-lā ḍ-ḍāllīn*' (*Jawhar*, 191).

120 That is, to say '*Samiʿa Llāhu li-man ḥamidah*' (Allah answers the one who praises Him) loudly in the standing after the bowing.

121 That is, regardless of whether the imam was in a loud or silent prayer.

122 This is to reply to the *tasmīʿ* by saying '*Rabbanā laka l-ḥamd*' (Our Lord, for You is praise) silently. The following are other slight variations which are also permissible to recite:

Rabbanā wa-laka l-ḥamd (Our Lord, and for You is praise)
Allāh-humma Rabbanā wa-laka l-ḥamd (O Allah, our Lord, and for You is praise)
Allāh-humma Rabbanā laka l-ḥamd (O Allah, our Lord, for You is praise). According to ʿAynī, this is the best expression (*Minḥa*, 137).

123 The one praying alone should say both the *tasmīʿ* and the *taḥmīd* in any prayer he prays.

when in the sitting position;[124] the women should do *tawarruk*[125]

124 With the toes of the right foot facing the *qibla*; on the authority of Ibn 'Umar who said, 'Of the sunnas of *salāh* is to keep the right foot upright [when sitting] and to direct it with the toes towards the *qibla*, and to sit on the left [buttock]' (*Sunan al-Nasā'ī al-Ṣughrā (al-Mujtabā)*, 2:236.1158).

125 *Tawarruk* is a manner of sitting. It is to place one's posterior on the floor whilst sitting mostly on the left buttock, with the thighs upon each other and the left foot protruding from underneath the right knee (*Jawhar*, 193; *Badā'i'*, 1:211).

CHAPTER 4

The Recommended (*Mustaḥabbāt*)

They [the recommended acts] are twenty-three.

The generic of them are fourteen:

1. Not turning right or left[126] – according to some[127]
2. To cover the mouth when yawning[128]
3. To stave off coughing as much as possible[129]

126 It is not clear what the author's intention is here as moving the neck is severely offensive in prayer. Unless he means not to turn the face right or left with minimal movement of the neck? All in all, it is recommended when standing to look at the place of one's prostration, when bowing to look at the feet, when prostrating to look at the tip of one's nose, when sitting to look at one's lap and when giving the *salāms* to look at the right and then left shoulder because the objective thereof is to achieve humility in prayer in a natural manner, and when someone is praying the eyes naturally look at these places (*Tabyīn*, 1:283; *Jawhar*, 193).

127 This statement is an indication that the author considers it questionable that this is from the recommended acts of prayer. In addition, he later mentions the same act from the unlawful acts (*al-Mirqāt*, 180).

128 The mouth can be covered with one's hand or sleeve. Sarakhsī states, 'When someone yawns in prayer it is desirable for him to cover his mouth, because not covering the mouth when speaking to people is considered bad etiquette, and thus when speaking to Allah it has greater priority' (*al-Mabsūṭ*, 1:44). One of the ways mentioned by the scholars to stave off yawning is to think in one's mind that the prophets never ever yawned; Qudūrī states, 'We have tried this on multiple occasions and we have found it so' (*Radd*, 2:155).

129 It is recommended to try and control the natural urge to cough as much as possible until one is no longer able in which case one is excused. One should not cough if there is no urge or need as this can invalidate the prayer as will be discussed later. Clearing one's throat to better one's recitation or to inform others that one is

4. To recite more than three verses[130]
5. Reciting in a beautiful manner[131]
6. For the head to be at the same level as the back when bowing[132]
7. To place one's knees [upon the floor] before the hands, and to place one's hands before the nose, and the nose before the forehead when prostrating
8. And the opposite [order] of that when getting up to stand
9. To prostrate between the hands[133]
10. To direct one's fingers and toes towards the *qibla*
11. Not wiping the forehead of any dirt and sweat before giving the *salāms*[134]
12. Leaving a gap of four fingers between the feet when standing[135]

---

in prayer is considered a valid excuse and does not invalidate the prayer according to the sounder opinion (*Radd*, 2:156).

130 That is, to read more than the *wājib* amount, which is either three short verses or one long verse, is considered sunna (*al-Mirqāt*, 181).

131 This is to comply with the rules of recitation or *tajwīd*, which if left would not result in a change in the structure of the word or its meaning; because to recite in a manner that does not change the meaning is not recommended but obligatory (*Jawhar*, 194).

132 Such that if a bowl of water were placed on the back it would not fall over. It is important to note that Shurunbulālī considered this from the sunnas of prayer and not from the recommended (*Marāqī*, 2:137; *Jawhar*, 194).

133 That is, for the head to be between the hands when prostrating, and the hands to be parallel to the ears such that if something were to fall off from the ears it would fall on the thumb (*Jawhar*, 194). It has been related from Wā'il b. Ḥujr that, 'When the Messenger of Allah ﷺ prostrated, he prostrated between his hands' (*Muslim*, 1:301.401).

134 Shaykhī Zāda mentions that the reason it is recommended is 'because it [wiping the forehead] is being busy with an act that is not appropriate in prayer, and [in addition, it is] removing the effect of prostration that gives rise to the feeling of being close to Allah Almighty' (*Majma' al-Anhur*, 1:159).

135 As this is what is more appropriate for achieving humility in prayer. Joining of the feet with wide gaps between the feet is not from the sunna and is a reprehensible innovation that should be stopped. It is very disheartening to see that the concentration of so many people in prayer is upon their feet and whether they are touching their neighbour's feet or not! These people claim to be following the hadiths; however, what is actually meant in the hadiths that mention the Companions 'joining heels with heels' in prayer is the act of congregating with each person

13. To place one's hands on the thighs when sitting[136]
14. To move one's head right and [then] left when giving the *salāms*[137]

The specific are nine:

1. To raise one's hands, at the places where it is considered sunna, to the level of one's earlobes for males; and up to the shoulders for females
2. To place the hands below the navel for males and on the chest for females[138]
3. To remove the palms from the sleeves for males when making the opening *takbīr*[139]
4. The imam's recitation to be the amount that has been transmitted[140]
5. To glorify an odd number, [but] more than three times for the one praying alone
6. For males to distance the upper arms from the flanks, and the abdomen from the thighs, the thighs from the shins, and the shins from the floor when bowing and prostrating;[141] and the opposite for females

---

standing side by side (*Radd*, 2:116).

136 Such that the ends of the fingers are at the knees (*Jawhar*, 195).

137 That is, to exaggerate in turning the head in such a way that one can see one's shoulders. Perhaps what is meant with regards to turning right and left mentioned in 'the sunnas' is to simply turn the head even if it is a very little amount (*al-Mirqāt*, 187).

138 The woman should simply place her right palm on the back of the left hand with the hands unclenched and straight.

139 Because this is considered closer to humility and furthest from resembling the way of tyrants. Females, however, should try and cover their palms to prevent the forearms, which are considered from their *'awra*, from being uncovered (*Marāqī*, 2:151).

140 That is, for the non-traveller to recite after the Fātiḥa in the *fajr* and *ẓuhr* prayers from the *ṭiwāl al-mufaṣṣal* (from Surat al-Ḥujurāt to Surat al-Burūj), in *'aṣr* and *'ishā'* from the *awsāṭ al-mufaṣṣal* (from Surat al-Burūj to Surat al-Bayyina) and in *maghrib* from the *qiṣār al-mufaṣṣal* (from Surat al-Bayyina to Surat al-Nās) as has been mentioned in certain narrations.

141 In the situation where one is praying in congregation and there is no space, one should not do this so that those praying next to one are not harmed in any way (*Jawhar*, 198).

7. To recite the Fātiḥa after the first two units for the one praying an obligatory prayer according to the well-known opinion[142]
8. To mention the name of Allah before the Fātiḥa in each unit[143]
9. For the latecomer to wait until the imam has completely finished [his prayer][144]

142 Rāzī states, 'The [recitation of the] Fātiḥa in the last two units is sunna; if one glorified in them, it is permissible, but it is offensive if one remained silent' (*Tuḥfa*, 107).

143 The sounder opinion, as mentioned previously, is that it is sunna to say the *basmala* at the start of every single unit.

144 That is, to wait until the imam has given the *salāms* twice, before standing up to complete the prayer.

CHAPTER 5

The Unlawful (*Muḥarramāt*)[145]

They [the unlawful acts] are fourteen in general:

1. To recite the *basmala* loudly[146]
2. To say '*Āmīn*' loudly[147]
3. Turning right and left by moving some of the face[148]
4. To look [up] at the sky[149]

---

145 Our esteemed teacher, Dr Ṣalāḥ Abūl-Ḥājj, mentions, with regards to the naming of this chapter as 'the unlawful', that 'the author has done a strange thing by creating a chapter on the unlawful acts in prayer because most of what he has mentioned does not exceed being offensive (*karāha*). If he kept to the way of the scholars of the school and placed them under "the offensive acts" then his book would be safe from being considered unreliable. Thus, the reader must be mindful and place this chapter and what is included in it among the offensive acts, so that he does not fall into problems' (*al-Mirqāt*, 190).

146 It is offensive – and not unlawful – to recite the *basmala*, regardless of whether it is a loud or a silent prayer, as this practice is considered contradictory to the sunna of the Messenger of Allah ﷺ (*Jawhar*, 207).

147 This is likewise offensive – and not unlawful – due to its being considered contradictory to the sunna.

148 This is considered severely offensive, but it does not nullify the prayer. On the authority of 'Ā'isha who said, 'I asked the Messenger of Allah ﷺ about looking here and there during the prayer. He replied, "It is what Satan steals from the prayer of any one of you"' (*Bukhārī*, 4:125.3291). And, in another hadith Anas relates that, 'The Messenger of Allah ﷺ said to me, "My son, beware of looking around in prayer, because looking around in prayer is [a cause of] destruction"' (*Tirmidhī*, 1:484.589). As for moving the chest away from the *qibla*, then this nullifies the prayer.

149 Anas relates that, 'The Messenger of Allah ﷺ said, "What is the matter with

5. To lean on a pillar, a hand or the like without an excuse[150]

6. To raise the hands at a place where it is not legislated[151]

7. To raise the toes from the floor when bowing and prostrating

8. Sitting on one's heels for the *tashahhud*[152]

9. Fiddling with one's clothes or body, less than three times[153]

10. To raise the index finger like the people of hadith[154]

---

people who look up at the sky when praying?!" He spoke sternly with regards to that until he said, "They must stop that, or they will certainly lose their eyesight'" (*Bukhārī*, 1:150.750).

150 That is, in an obligatory prayer. It is not offensive in a supererogatory prayer.

151 For example, before or after the bowing, as it is considered a surplus act. However, because the act is something that is found in prayer then the prayer is not invalidated, but it is considered offensive (*Jawhar*, 210).

152 This is one of the understandings of *al-iq'ā'* or 'squatting like a dog', whose prohibition has been mentioned in certain narrations. Sarakhsī states, 'There are two explanations with regards to understanding [the word] *al-iq'ā'*. The first one is [that it means] to raise both feet, like one does when prostrating and to put both buttocks on one's heels' (*al-Mabsūṭ*, 1:31).

153 *Al-'abath* or fiddling/fidgeting in prayer, like playing with one's beard, clothes or fingers, is considered severely offensive; it has been related that the Messenger of Allah ﷺ said, 'Allah has disliked for you to fiddle in prayer' (*Musnad al-Shihāb*, 2:155.1087).

The author has stipulated 'less than three times' to distinguish between excessive movement (*'amal kathīr*) and non-excessive movements, as according to some scholars in the school three or more movements are considered excessive and will nullify the prayer. However, even though this opinion has a strong basis, it is contrary to the more relied-upon position, as will be discussed later.

154 This is one of the rulings that has been criticised in this book and is in need of further clarification. There are three opinions with regards to pointing with the index finger in the *tashahhud*:

1. To place the hands on the thighs with the fingers pointing towards the *qibla* and *not* pointing with the index finger at all

2. To do the same as no. 1, but to raise the index finger whilst clasping the ring and little finger and making a ring with the thumb and middle finger when reaching the words '*lā ilāha*', and to lower it when saying '*illā Llāh*'

3. To do the same as no. 2, but without clasping the fingers

The first opinion is what many of the authors of the manuals of Sacred Law (*mutūn*) like the *Hidāya*, *Kanz al-Daqā'iq*, *Mukhtṣar al-Qudūrī* and *Tanwīr* opine. However, later scholars like Ibn 'Ābidīn and Ibn al-Humām felt the second opinion to

11. Restricting the *salām* to only one side[155]
12. Performing the *qunūt* in other than the *witr* [prayer][156]
13. Adding to the *takbīr*, praise (*thanā'*), glorifications (*tasbīḥāt*) or *tashahhud*[157] over and above the sunna amount[158]
14. Neglecting any *wājib* – which has been mentioned previously – deliberately[159]

And, in *al-Muḥīṭ*[160] he has mentioned the unlawful acts in the [chapter of the] offensive.[161]

---

be more correct. All in all, all three opinions have been validated by scholars in the madhhab and so it is unbecoming of the author to describe raising the finger as being unlawful and specific to the people of hadith. This is why 'Abd al-Ghanī al-Nābulsī mentions that it should not even be considered offensive; and even if it were considered offensive, it should be no more than slightly offensive (*Jawhar*, 211; *Minnat al-Fattāḥ*, 1:177; *Radd*, 2:191–193; *al-Mirqāt*, 186–187).

155 Because to say the *salāms* twice is necessary as mentioned previously.

156 The *qunūt* supplication is only performed in prayers other than the *witr* when there is a huge calamity that has befallen the people, in which case it can be performed in every single prayer. If someone is praying behind an imam who is performing the *qunūt* in another prayer (e.g. *fajr*), then one should simply stand silently (*Jawhar*, 212).

157 It is severely offensive to recite anything other than the *tashhahud* of Ibn Mas'ūd outlined previously. Sending salutations after the *tashahhud* in the first sitting is also considered severely offensive, as it is considered to be adding to the *tashhahud* (*Jawhar*, 213).

158 For example, to say '*Allāh akbar wa-a'ẓam*' when reciting the *takbīr*, to add '*Wa-jalla thanā'uka wa-taqaddasat asmā'uka*' when reciting the *thanā'* or adding '*Subḥāna Rabbī al-a'lā al-wahhāb*' when glorifying in the prostrations. To do so is considered slightly offensive and its offensiveness stems from the contradiction of the sunna therein. However, this ruling is specific to obligatory prayers – there is no blame if this is performed in a supererogatory prayer (*Jawhar*, 212–213).

159 This is severely offensive and it becomes necessary to repeat the prayer in the prayer time as has been mentioned previously.

160 That is, *al-Muḥīṭ al-Burhānī* of Muḥammad b. Aḥmad b. Mādha al-Bukhārī.

161 The author is recognising the fact that the rulings mentioned here are in reality mostly offensive, but because many of them are severely offensive, and the severely offensive according to Muḥammad b. al-Ḥasan al-Shaybānī is considered unlawful, it could explain why he chose to name this chapter 'the unlawful' – that is, as a way of distinguishing between the severely and slightly offensive (*Jawhar*, 214).

CHAPTER 6

The Offensive (*Makrūhāt*)

They [the offensive acts] are fifty-nine. The generic [of them] are forty-two:

1. Repeating the *takbīr*[162]
2. Counting verses [of the Qur'an] and the like[163] using one's hand[164]
3. Putting the hands on the hips[165]
4. [To do] anything that is considered from the way of the haughty[166]
5. To clear the throat without an excuse, if it is done without pronouncing any letters[167]

---

162 For example, to say '*Allāh akbar*' twice. Doing this is considered slightly offensive (*Jawhar*, 215).

163 For example, glorifications or any transmitted supplications of prayer (*Jawhar*, 215).

164 Counting verses of the Qur'an in one's heart or by gentle pressure on the fingers is permissible without any disagreement and is not what is intended here. What is meant here is to count by moving the fingers or by holding something in the hand; to do this is considered slightly offensive as it is not from the actions of prayer and contradicts the concept of displaying humility therein (*Nuzhat al-Fikr*, 65–75).

165 As this is contrary to the sunna; on the authority of Abū Hurayra who said, 'The Messenger of Allah ﷺ forbade for a man to pray with his hands on the hips' (*Muslim*, 2:67.1220).

166 That is, to do something that is from the manner of the arrogant and vainglorious, e.g. raising the clothes when prostrating so that they do not become dusty, or to place a handkerchief to prostrate upon (*Jawhar*, 218).

167 It is offensive because if speech is produced with the sound of two syllables, then the prayer is nullified (*Majma' al-Anhur*, 1:151).

6. Expelling mucus [without an excuse][168]
7. Expelling air inaudibly[169]
8. To hold dirhams or the like in the mouth such that the recitation is not prevented[170]
9. To raise the head when bowing[171]
10. Swallowing anything between the teeth, if it was small[172]
11. Neglecting any of the sunnas[173]
12. To finish the recitation in the *rukūʿ*[174]
13. For the remembrances to happen while moving from one position to another[175]
14. To place one's hands before the knees on the floor when prostrating without an excuse
15. And to raise them after the knees when standing likewise[176]
16. To squat like a dog[177]

---

168 The same rulings with regards to clearing the throat are also applied to this issue.

169 Kāsānī states, 'It is offensive to expel air in prayer because it is not from the actions of prayer and there is no need therein, as opposed to taking a breath, for there is a need in this. And does expelling air nullify the prayer? If it is inaudible, then it does not nullify [it], but if it is audible, then it does according to Abū Ḥanīfa and Muḥammad [al-Shaybānī]' (*Badāʾiʿ*, 1:218).

170 In which case it is slightly offensive. However, if it prevents one from pronouncing any of the letters, then it is impermissible (*Durr* and *Radd*, 2:351).

171 That is, to raise it higher than one's posterior.

172 Anything the size of a dry chickpea or smaller is considered 'small' in legal terms, and anything bigger than a dry chickpea is considered 'large'. Swallowing a food particle in the mouth that is 'small' is excused but slightly offensive. However, swallowing a 'large' particle nullifies the prayer (*Jawhar*, 220).

173 That is, any of the sunnas mentioned in Chapter 3.

174 That is, finishing off any *wājib* or sunna recitation whilst still bowing. Finishing off any obligatory recitation in this state is impermissible and will nullify the prayer (*Jawhar*, 220).

175 For example, to finish the glorifications of the bowing whilst standing back up.

176 That is, if this is done without a valid excuse. There is no blame if it is done in the presence of a valid excuse.

177 *Al-iqʿāʾ* or to squat is to sit on the buttocks with the knees raised, bringing them in to the chest and placing the hands on the floor (*al-Mabsūṭ*, 1:31; *Ḥalabī*

17. To cover the mouth without being overcome with yawning[178]

18. To close the eyes [completely][179]

19. Moving stones; except if one could not [otherwise] prostrate and thus did it once or twice[180]

20. Wiping the dirt or sweat off one's forehead before finishing the prayer[181]

21. To gather [one's] clothing[182]

Kabīr, 346). Abū Hurayra relates that the Messenger of Allah ﷺ said, 'My Beloved counselled me with three things and forbade me with three. He counselled me with [performing] the *witr* [prayer] before sleep, fasting three days of each month and [performing] two units of the *ḍuḥā* [prayer]. And, He forbade me from looking around [in prayer], squatting like a dog and pecking like a rooster' (*Musnad Aḥmad*, 13:38.7595).

178 It is from good etiquette to stave off yawning as much as possible, and only when one is overcome should one place a hand or the like over the mouth (*Badā'i'*, 1:215).

179 On the authority of Ibn 'Abbās who said, 'The Messenger of Allah ﷺ said, "If any one of you stands for prayer, then do not close your eyes"' (*al-Mu'jam al-Kabīr*, 11:34.10956).
Kāsānī states, 'It is offensive to close the eyes in prayer because of what has been related from the Messenger of Allah ﷺ, that he forbade closing the eyes in prayer, and [also] because the sunna is to keep one's gaze at the place of [one's] prostration and in closing the eyes there is neglect of this sunna. But also, because every single limb is due a portion of this worship, and so too the eyes' (*Badā'i'*, 1:216). However, it is generally agreed that closing the eyes is permissible if doing so allows one to concentrate more in prayer and helps one achieve humility; although, one should try and only do it when the need arises and not all the time (*Marāqī*, 2:260).

180 If one cannot place the head on the floor for the minimal obligatory amount without needing to move something out of the way, then it is permissible to move it, but it should only be done once or twice, with some scholars, like Ḥalabī, preferring doing it once only 'and not more than that because of the statement of the Messenger of Allah ﷺ "do not touch pebbles whilst you are praying; but, if you must, then do it once"' (*Ḥalabī Kabīr*, 350).

181 If there is benefit therein, e.g. if the sweat was entering the eye and causing pain, then it is permissible to wipe it as it helps the heart to concentrate on the prayer (*Ḥalabī Kabīr*, 357).

182 That is, it is offensive to pull the end of one's garment up from the front or back when prostrating to stop it from getting dirty as it is considered a form of arrogance and haughtiness. In the same manner as tucking one's garment, it is also offensive to fold one's sleeves or trousers when praying for it too is considered a form of arrogance (*al-Mabsūṭ*, 1:38; *al-Mirqāt*, 195; *Jawhar*, 223).

22. Yawning[183]
23. To stretch one's limbs[184]
24. Cracking one's knuckles[185]
25. Swaying side to side[186]
26. To spread out the fingers in [any place] other than the bowing
27. Hastening in the recitation[187]
28. Not keeping the head straight with the back when bowing
29. Taking three or more steps without an excuse as long as one paused a brief moment after each step[188]

---

183 On the authority of Abū Hurayra who said, 'The Messenger of Allah ﷺ said, "Yawning in prayer is from Satan, and so, if any one of you yawns, then try and suppress it as much as possible"' (*Tirmidhī*, 2:206.370).

184 On the authority of Abū Hurayra who said, 'The Messenger of Allah ﷺ forbade for a man to stretch his limbs in prayer or [to stretch them] in front of women; except [if it was done] in front of his wife or slave-girl' (Dāraquṭnī's *al-Afrād*, cited in *al-Jāmiʿ al-Ṣaghīr*, 2:478).

185 On the authority of ʿAlī who said, 'The Messenger of Allah ﷺ said, "Do not crack your knuckles whilst you are in prayer"' (*Sunan Ibn Māja*, 1:310.965). Ibn ʿAbidīn states, 'And it [cracking the knuckles] should be considered severely offensive' (*Radd*, 2:353).

186 Because it is considered frivolous, which is contrary to displaying humility in prayer (*Jawhar*, 224).

187 That is, to the point where one can just about recite the letters properly (*Jawhar*, 224).

188 Walking in prayer is of two types:

1. Without an excuse
If one walks 'excessively' – defined as three or more steps – without pausing between each step, then the prayer is nullified, even if one did not turn away from the *qibla*. If it was an excessive amount but not continuous (i.e. one stopped between each step for a brief moment), then it will not nullify the prayer but is considered offensive.

2. With an excuse
For example, nullifying one's *wuḍū'* in prayer and going to perform it anew, or performing a prayer in the presence of fear. In these circumstances, walking three or more steps is *not* nullifying or offensive, even if one turned away from the *qibla*. If one moved for another excuse than what has been mentioned (i.e. *wuḍū'* or fear), then the prayer is nullified if one turned away from the *qibla* regardless of how many steps one took. If one did not turn away from the *qibla*, then walking a small amount is not nullifying or offensive, but if it is an excessive amount without stopping, then the prayer is nullified (*Durr* and *Radd*, 2:335–336).

30. To sway right and left
31. To kill a louse in less than three movements[189]
32. And to bury it likewise[190]
33. To spit out saliva[191]
34. To remove footgear[192] with minimal movement[193]
35. To smell scent[194]
36. To fan [oneself] with [one's] clothing or a fan less than three times[195]
37. To appoint a sura for a specific prayer such that one does not recite anything else[196]
38. To combine between two suras by omitting one [sura] between

---

189 And likewise, any other similar insect. It is offensive to take, kill or remove the insect if it is not causing any harm. If, however, the louse or insect is being harmful to the person whilst in prayer and one is outside the mosque, then it is not considered offensive to kill it; however, Abū Ḥanīfa preferred burying it under a stone, for example, and considered it offensive to kill it. However, if one is in the mosque, and the insect is being harmful, then there is no offense in killing it, but one should not fling it away or bury it except if one is sure that one will be able to retrieve it after finishing the prayer (*Radd*, 2:366).

190 That is, in less than three movements.

191 It is offensive if there is no need to do so. If, however, there is a need, then one can spit it out under one's left foot – which is, of course, if one is praying in other than the mosque. Although, better than all of this is to use a tissue or the hem of one's clothes (*Ḥalabī Kabīr*, 356).

192 That is, footgear that has not been wiped over, as removing footgear that has been wiped over nullifies the prayer.

193 And likewise, a hat, shirt or any other similar attire.

194 That is, to actively sniff it. It does not mean to merely smell fragrance or perfume in the air (*Jawhar*, 226).

195 That is, less than three continual movements, as three continual movements are generally considered excessive and will nullify the prayer (*Ḥalabī Kabīr*, 357).

196 Ibn al-Humām states, 'The truth is, doing it persistently (*mudāwama*) is unconditionally offensive, regardless of whether one believed it to be compulsory and offensive to read other than it, or not. Because, the evidence of its offensiveness … is giving the suggestion of favouritism and abandoning the rest [of the Qur'an] … Rather, it is recommended to recite it sometimes as a way of seeking blessings with that which has been narrated, as the possibility of suggesting [favouritism] is removed by leaving [its recitation] sometimes' (*Fatḥ*, 1:337).

them, in one unit[197]

39. To move from one verse to another, even if there was a sura between them[198]

40. To give precedence to a later sura over an early sura, even if done over two units[199]

41. To say the *basmala* before every sura in each unit[200]

42. To lift a child without an excuse[201]

The specific are seventeen:

---

197 It is offensive to combine, regardless of the number of suras left, between the two suras in one unit. As for combining between the units, then if there are two suras or more between them, it is not offensive. If there is only one sura between them, then it has been said that it is offensive, but it has also been opined that if it is a long sura, then it is not offensive just like if there were two small suras between them (*Fatḥ*, 1:343).

198 This includes moving from one verse in one sura to another verse in a different sura or omitting verses in the same sura (*Fatḥ*, 1:343).

199 For example, if one recited Surat al-Fīl in the first unit and Surat al-Naba' in the second unit. It has been said, however, that this is offensive only if it is done deliberately; if it is done by mistake or because of a valid excuse, then it is not considered offensive (*Jawhar*, 228).

200 According to Abū Ḥanīfa and Abū Yūsuf, the *basmala* is not recited before the sura that is recited after the Fātiḥa, because it is not a verse from the beginning of the sura. According to Muḥammad al-Shaybanī, however, one should recite it before the sura in a silent prayer, but not in a loud prayer. If one did recite it in a loud prayer, then there should be a pause between the Fātiḥa and sura so one can say it silently. In reality, the difference of opinion arises due to trying to understand what is regarded as the sunna in this matter. Therefore, there is *no* offense in implementing either opinion, although the opinion of Abū Ḥanīfa is what many of the scholars have preferred and verified (*al-Mirqāt*, 199).

201 As for what has been narrated by Abū Qatāda who said, 'The Messenger of Allah ﷺ was praying while holding Umāma, the daughter of Zaynab [the daughter of the Messenger of Allah ﷺ] and Abūl-'Āṣ b. al-Rabī'. When he stood, he would lift her and when he prostrated, he would put her down' (*Muslim*, 1:385.543), then the scholars interpret this hadith in multiple ways. The first is that there was a need to hold her because there was no one available to look after her and secondly, to show that this action is permissible and does not break the prayer if there is a need. Some have also mentioned that the above hadith is abrogated by the hadith 'verily, the prayer demands one's whole attention' although Ibn 'Ābidīn rejects this possibility as the hadith of Umāma occurred after this hadith (*Radd*, 2:367).

1. The imam waiting in prayer for the one whose footsteps he can hear[202]
2. To lengthen the second [unit] more than the first [unit] in obligatory prayers[203]
3. To pause at verses of mercy and punishment for [both] the imam and follower without exception, and for the one praying alone in obligatory prayers[204]
4. To prostrate on the coil of the turban[205]
5. For men to join the abdomen to the thighs [when prostrating][206]
6. And likewise, for them to lay down the forearms [against the floor][207]
7. And for them to take off a shirt or hat, or to don them with minimal movements

202 Abūl-Layth al-Samarqandī mentions regarding this issue that, 'if the imam knows the one coming, then he should not wait because it resembles having an inclination [in prayer to someone other than Allah]; if he did not know him, then it is okay because that entails aiding [someone] in worship' (*Badā'i'*, 1:209; *Jawhar*, 230).

203 It is slightly offensive if the second sura is longer by more than three verses if the verses of the two suras are of similar length; otherwise, it is the quantity of words/letters which are of significance such that if one read twenty long verses in the first unit and twenty short verses in the second whose words were equivalent to approximately half of what was read in the first unit, then the sunna has been achieved. There is a difference of opinion with regards to supererogatory prayers; according to Tumurtāshī there is no offensiveness, whereas Shurunbulālī considers the sounder position to be that it is offensive (*Tanwīr*, *Durr* and *Radd*, 2:233–235; *Marāqī*, 2:255; *Ḥalabī Kabīr*, 355).

204 That is, to pause to ask for mercy or forgiveness as it disrupts the obligation of listening to the Qur'an when it is being recited. In a supererogatory prayer, however, one is allowed to supplicate when reading verses of paradise, hell, forgiveness and the like (*al-Mirqāt*, 200).

205 It is permissible – but offensive when there is no need to prostrate on the coil of a turban – as long as the turban was on the forehead. Otherwise, the prostration will be deemed invalid. In the presence of a need, e.g. if the earth is too hot or too cold, then there is no offense (*Jawhar*, 230; *al-Mirqāt*, 201).

206 Except if there is congestion and overcrowdedness in the lines of prayer, in which case it is not offensive (*Jawhar*, 231).

207 That is, one should make sure the forearms are not touching the ground when prostrating. It has been said that is offensive because it is a trait of laziness and of being neglectful; in addition to the resemblance therein of predatory animals and dogs (*Radd*, 2:355).

8. For the imam to lengthen the prayer to an extent that it becomes cumbersome upon the congregation[208]
9. And to hasten it [likewise] for those of them who are in a hurry[209]
10. For the imam to seek rectification from the congregation if he has already read an amount with which the prayer is valid[210]
11. To pray supererogatory prayers in the day loudly[211]
12. For the imam to recite a verse of prostration in a silent prayer except if at the end of the sura[212]
13. Repeating a verse out of joy or sadness in obligatory prayers without an excuse, except in supererogatory or sunna prayers unconditionally[213]

---

208 That is, by increasing upon the sunna amount mentioned previously. 'Abd al-Ghanī al-Nābulsī felt that this is severely offensive due to the prohibition mentioned in the hadith of Jābir b. 'Abdullāh where he states, 'Mu'ādh b. Jabal would pray with the Messenger of Allah ﷺ and then go to lead his people in prayer. Once, he led the people in prayer and recited Surat al-Baqara. A man left [the rows] and offered a short prayer [separately] and went away. When Mu'ādh came to know about this, he said. "He is a hypocrite!" The man heard this; and so he came to the Messenger of Allah ﷺ and said, "Messenger of Allah ﷺ! We are people who work with our hands and irrigate [our farms] with our camels. Last night Mu'ādh led us in prayer and he recited Surat al-Baqara and so I offered my prayer separately. Because of this, he accused me of being a hypocrite." The Messenger of Allah ﷺ called Mu'ādh and said [to him] thrice, "Mu'ādh! Are you a troublemaker?! Recite [instead], '*Wa-sh-shamsi wa-ḍuḥāhā*' [Q 91], '*Sabbiḥi sma Rabbika l-a'lā*' [Q 87] and the like"' (*Bukhārī*, 1:26.6106; *Jawhar*, 238).

209 That is, to hasten it in such a way that the sunnas are not performed (*Jawhar*, 238).

210 That is, after praying a sufficient amount, instead of bowing the imam waits to be corrected by someone from the congregation; however, it is important to note that this does not nullify the prayer of the imam or the one who is making the correction (*al-Mirqāt*, 202).

211 As the supererogatory prayers follow the obligatory prayers with regards to the rulings of reciting loudly or silently.

212 That is, it is not offensive if the verse of prostration is the last thing recited and then one immediately bows, because bowing can act as a substitute for the prostration (*Jawhar*, 233).

213 That is, in a supererogatory or sunna prayer one can repeat a verse of the Qur'an with or without an excuse. It has been related that the Messenger of Allah ﷺ stood the entire night repeating, '*And if You punish them, they are Your servants*' (Q 5:118), and likewise it has been related that Ibn Mas'ūd stood the entire night

14. To repeat a sura in one unit in obligatory prayers[214]
15. For males to pray with the sleeves folded up to the elbows[215]
16. For the one praying behind the imam to say, 'Allah has spoken the truth and His messengers have relayed,' at a verse that incites yearning or instils fear[216]
17. To lean on a wall, pillar or the like without an excuse in other than the supererogatory prayers

---

repeating, '*but say, "Lord, increase me in knowledge!"*' (Q 20:114) (*Jawhar*, 233).

214 And likewise, it is offensive to repeat a sura by reciting it in the second unit if one was capable of reciting another – otherwise, it is not. It is also not offensive if it happened forgetfully or by mistake, e.g. if one recited Surat al-Nās in the first unit, then it is not offensive to recite it again in the second (*Jawhar*, 234).

215 That is, if one folded the sleeves outside of prayer and *then* started the prayer. Folding them whilst in prayer will nullify the prayer as it is excessive movement. The 'elbows' are mentioned here, because normally it is up to this point that the sleeves are folded up. However, what is correct in this matter is that praying with folded sleeves, regardless of how much one folds, is considered offensive. Folding the trousers follows the same ruling as folding the sleeves (*Radd*, 2:350).

216 As this interferes with the obligation of listening to the Qur'an (*Jawhar*, 234).

CHAPTER 7

The Permissible (*Mubāḥāt*)

They [the permissible acts] are eleven.

The generic [of them] are eight:

1. To look with one's peripheral vision without turning the face[217]
2. To make suitable the place of one's prostration [if done] once or twice due to a need[218]
3. To kill a freely wandering snake, in all circumstances, even if [killing] it needed [some type of] manipulation[219]
4. To keep [some] dirhams or dinars in one's mouth in a way that does not prevent one from performing the sunna [amount of] recitation[220]
5. To have in one's hand that which does not prevent one from [upholding] the sunnas related to keeping [one's] support [in

217 That is, without turning the neck. However, according to some it is slightly offensive or considered 'leaving the preferred' (*khilāf al-awlā*) to do so without a need (*Jawhar*, 201; *Durr* and *Radd*, 2:354).

218 That is, it is permissible to remove any objects like stones or pebbles that would hinder placing the full forehead on the ground when prostrating. However, it is only permissible with one or two movements. All in all, it is better to leave it if one is able to place most of the forehead on the ground (*Durr* and *Radd*, 2:352).

219 Killing a snake, scorpion or any harmful creature in prayer is allowed unconditionally (i.e. even if it needed excessive movement) and does not nullify the prayer. Abū Hurayra relates that the Messenger of Allah ﷺ said, 'Kill the two black things in prayer: the snake and the scorpion' (*Abū Dāwūd*, 2:185.921; *Radd*, 2:364–365).

220 This also includes keeping anything in the mouth that does not disintegrate.

prayer][221]

6. To recite the Qur'an by combining [the suras][222]
7. To shake [one's] clothing so that it does not stick to one's body when bowing
8. To read the end of a sura in one unit and the end of another [sūra] in another [unit] according to the sounder position

The specific are three:

1. To repeat a sura [or a verse] in one unit in a supererogatory prayer
2. To lean on a wall or pillar in a supererogatory prayer, even if [done] without an excuse
3. For the imam to observe those behind him because of doubt [in the number of units prayed] – that is, he stands if they stand and so on[223]

---

221 For example, placing the right hand over the left when reciting, or holding both knees when in *rukūʿ*.

222 That is, to combine multiple suras in the order of composition in one unit or prayer (*al-Mirqāt*, 205).

223 That is, to glance at the congregation behind, with one's peripheral vision, if one is doubtful and hesitant in whether one should remain sitting or standing (*al-Mirqāt*, 206).

CHAPTER 8

The Nullifiers (*Mufsidāt*)

The more precise [opinion][224] is that they [the nullifiers] are five in general:

1. To speak[225] with [what is considered] human speech in all circumstances,[226] whether [it is human speech defined] in real (*ḥaqīqatan*) or legal (*ḥukman*) terms[227]

---

224 That is, these five are considered the primary nullifiers of prayer. Other nullifying acts generally fall under one of these five categories.

225 Speech is the pronunciation of two or more letters that at the very least can be heard by the person himself or have the capacity to be heard if an obstacle, e.g. deafness or a loud sound, was removed (*Jawhar*, 236).

226 That is, regardless of whether it is done deliberately, by mistake, in a conscious state or when unconscious. This applies to all nullifiers of prayer – the mere presence of a nullifying act invalidates the prayer without any consideration of other factors.

227 'Human speech' (*kalām al-nās*) is any speech that contains a request which can be granted by people (i.e. as opposed to something that can only be granted by Allah). If this speech is directed to a person, then it is real human speech, e.g. if one said to another person, 'Give me a hundred pounds.' But, if this type of speech is directed to Allah, e.g. if someone said, 'O Allah, give me a hundred pounds,' then it is considered human speech in legal terms. Both real and legal speech nullify the prayer. As for speaking in prayer that is not considered 'human speech', like asking Allah for mercy or forgiveness, then this does not invalidate the prayer.
Mu'āwiya b. al-Ḥakam relates that the Messenger of Allah ﷺ said, 'Verily this prayer, nothing of the speech of man is appropriate in it; verily, it is glorifications, exaltations and recitation of the Qur'an' (*Muslim*, 1:381.537); and in another hadith Zayd b. al-Arqam relates that, 'We used to talk while engaged in prayer and a person talked with a companion next to him in prayer until it was revealed, "*And stand before Allah in devout obedience*" [Q 2:238], and thus we were commanded to observe silence [in prayer] and were forbidden to speak' (*Muslim*, 1:383.539).

2. Quiet laughter (*ḍaḥik*)[228]

3. Excessive movement that is not for the purpose of repairing [the prayer][229]

4. Neglecting an obligatory act of prayer without an excuse, even if it was missed unexpectedly without the desire to do so

5. Deliberately bringing about ritual impurity[230]

Included in human speech is to say anything with the purpose of answering (*ijāba*), e.g. supplicating for the one who sneezes, replying to good news by saying '*al-Ḥamdu li-Llāh*' or replying to a question by reciting a verse of the Qur'an. However, if by saying '*al-Ḥamdu li-Llāh*' or '*Subḥāna Llāh*' one intended to inform others that one is in prayer, then it does not nullify the prayer (*Durr*, 2:318–329; *Jawhar*, 336; *Marāqī*, 2:217–220).

228 Quiet laughter is what can only be heard by the one praying himself. This type of laughter nullifies the prayer but not the *wuḍū'*. Loud laughter (*qahqaha*) is laughter than can be heard by those standing around a person; this type of laughter nullifies both the *wuḍū' and* the prayer as long as the person praying is not sleeping, is an adult and is in a prayer that involves both bowing and prostrating. As for smiling (*tabassum*), then this nullifies neither the *wuḍū'* nor the prayer (*Marāqī*, 1:376–377).

229 According to the more correct opinion, excessive movement is that which if an onlooker were to observe the one praying do (without any prior context), he would think that the person is not in prayer. This type of movement nullifies the prayer, unless it is done for the purpose of 'repairing' or restoring the prayer, e.g. walking to perform *wuḍū'* or killing a free snake, as mentioned previously. In these instances, excessive movement is excused, and the prayer is not nullified (*Marāqī*, 2:221; *Durr* and *Radd*, 2:332).

230 For example, passing wind or making oneself bleed. It is important to note that the prayer is nullified only if this happens before sitting the length of the *tashahhud* in the final sitting; after this, nullifying the *wuḍū' deliberately* is considered 'exiting the prayer with one's own act', and therefore the prayer would have been fulfilled but considered severely deficient due to the neglect of a *wājib* act of exiting the prayer with the *salāms*. It is also important to mention here that if someone nullified their *wuḍū'* in prayer unintentionally, then he has the option to do one of two things: (1) leave the prayer, perform *wuḍū'* and recontinue the prayer from where it was left, or (2) restart the prayer all together (which is the safer option) (*al-Mirqāt*, 209; *Radd*, 2:310).

APPENDIX A

The Obligatory Components of Prayer and a Summary of Their Rulings

See table on p. 74

	Farḍ	***Wājib***	**Sunna**	***Mustaḥabb***
The opening *takbīr* (*takbīr al-taḥrīma*)	A sincere word of remembrance (*dhikr khāliṣ*)	To say '*Allāhu akbar*'	To raise the hands	To raise the hands adjacent to the earlobes, while keeping the fingers outstretched in a normal manner
The standing (*qiyām*)	To stand in a manner whereby the fingertips of the hands cannot reach the knees		To have a straight back and to place the right hand over the left hand	For men to place the hands under the navel and for women to place them on the chest
The recitation (*qirā'a*)	Abū Ḥanīfa: one verse *Ṣāḥibayn*: one long verse or three short verses	The Fātiḥa and either a sura, three short verses or one long verse	To recite in a beautiful manner and to recite more than three verses	To recite from the *ṭiwāl al-mufaṣṣal* in *fajr* and *ẓuhr*, from the *awsāṭ al-mufaṣṣal* in *'aṣr* and *'ishā'* and the *qiṣār al-mufaṣṣal* in *maghrib*
The bowing (*rukū'*)	To bow to such an extent that it is possible for the fingertips to touch the knees	To have composure	To keep the back straight; to glorify thrice; to place the hands on the knees; to widen the fingers when grasping the knees; to keep the head at the same level as the back	To keep one's gaze on the toes
The prostration (*sajda*)	For the forehead to touch the ground	Composure and for the upper part of the nose to touch the ground	For the hands, knees and feet to touch the ground and to glorify thrice	To keep the hands facing the *qibla*
The last sitting (*al-qa'dat al-akhīra*)	To sit the length it takes to recite the *tashahhud*	The recitation of the *tashahhud*	The *Ṣalāt al-Ibrāhīmiyya*, supplication, and to place the hands on the thighs	For the fingertips to be at the edge of the knees when placing the hands on the thighs
Exiting with one's own act (*al-khurūj bi-ṣun'ihī*)	To perform any act that nullifies the prayer *after* the last sitting	To say '*al-salām*' twice	To add "*alaykum wa-raḥmat Allāh*' and to turn the head right and then left	To keep one's gaze on the shoulders when giving the *salāms*

APPENDIX B

Supplications

THE THANĀ'

سُبْحَانَكَ اللَّهُمَّ وَبِحَمْدِكَ وَتَبَارَكَ اسْمُكَ وَتَعَالَى جَدُّكَ وَلا إِلَهَ غَيْرُكَ

Subḥānaka Llāh-humma wa-bi-ḥamdika wa-tabāraka smuka wa-taʿālā jadduka wa-lā ilāha ghayruk(a).

'Glory be to You, O Allah, with Your praise. Blessed is Your Name; exalted is Your honour. There is no deity besides You.'

THE TASHAHHUD

التَّحِيَّاتُ للهِ وَالصَّلوَاتُ وَالطَّيِّبَاتُ، السَّلامُ عَلَيْكَ أَيُّهَا النَّبِيُّ
ورَحْمَةُ اللهِ وبَرَكَاتُهُ، السَّلامُ عَلَيْنَا وَعَلَى عِبَادِ اللهِ الصَّالِحِينَ،
أَشْهَدُ أنْ لا إِلَهَ إلا اللهُ وَأَشْهَدُ أَنَّ مُحَمَّداً عَبْدُهُ وَرَسُولُهُ

At-taḥiyyātu li-Llāhi wa-ṣ-ṣalawātu wa-ṭ-ṭayyibāt(u), as-salāmu ʿalayka ayyuha n-nabiyyu wa-raḥmatu Llāhi wa-barakātuh(u), as-salāmu ʿalaynā wa-ʿalā ʿibādi Llāhi ṣ-ṣāliḥīn, ashhadu an lā ilāha illā Llāhu wa-ashhadu anna Muḥammadan ʿabduhu wa-rasūluh(u).

'Greetings are for Allah, as well as prayers and all things pure. Peace be upon you, O Prophet, as well as the mercy of Allah and His blessings. Peace be upon us, and all the righteous servants of Allah. I bear witness that there is no deity except Allah, and I bear witness that Muhammad is His servant and messenger.'

THE ṢALĀT AL-IBRĀHĪMIYYA

اللَّهُمَّ صَلِّ عَلَى مُحَمَّدٍ وَعَلَى آلِ مُحَمَّدٍ، كَمَا صَلَّيْتَ عَلَى إِبْرَاهِيمَ، وَعَلَى آلِ إِبْرَاهِيمَ، إِنَّكَ حَمِيدٌ مَجِيدٌ، اللَّهُمَّ بَارِكْ عَلَى مُحَمَّدٍ وَعَلَى آلِ مُحَمَّدٍ، كَمَا بَارَكْتَ عَلَى إِبْرَاهِيمَ، وَعَلَى آلِ إِبْرَاهِيمَ، إِنَّكَ حَمِيدٌ مَجِيدٌ

Allāh-humma ṣalli 'alā Muḥammadin wa-'alā ālī Muḥammadin kamā ṣallayta 'alā Ibrāhīma wa-'alā ālī Ibrāhīm(a), innaka ḥamīdun majīd. Allāh-humma bārik 'alā Muḥammadin wa-'alā ālī Muḥammadin kamā bārakta 'alā Ibrāhīma wa-'alā ālī Ibrāhīm(a), innaka ḥamīdun majīd.

'O Allah! Send mercy upon Muhammad and upon the family of Muhammad just as You sent mercy upon Ibrāhīm and upon the family of Ibrahim. Verily, You are praiseworthy and majestic. O Allah! Send blessings upon Muhammad and upon the family of Muhammad just as You sent blessings upon Ibrahim and upon the family of Ibrahim. Verily, You are praiseworthy and majestic.'

SOME SUPPLICATIONS ONE CAN USE IN THE LAST SITTING OF PRAYER

رَبَّنَآ ءَاتِنَا فِي ٱلدُّنيَا حَسَنَةً وَفِي ٱلآخِرَةِ حَسَنَةً وَقِنَا عَذَابَ ٱلنَّارِ

Rabbanā ātinā fī d-dunyā ḥasana(tan), wa-fī l-ākhirati ḥasana(tan), wa-qinā 'adhāba n-nār.

'Our Lord, give us good in this world and in the hereafter, and protect us from the torment of the fire.'

رَبَّنَا ٱغْفِرْ لَنَا ذُنُوبَنَا وَإِسرَافَنَا فِيٓ أَمْرِنَا وَثَبِّتْ أَقْدَامَنَا
وَٱنْصُرْنَا عَلَى ٱلْقَوْمِ ٱلْكَٰفِرِينَ

Rabbanā ghfir lanā dhunūbanā wa-isrāfanā fī amrinā, wa-thabbit aqdāmanā, wa-nṣurnā ʿalā l-qawmi l-kāfirīn.

'Our Lord, forgive us our sins and our excesses. Make our feet firm, and give us help against the disbelievers.'

رَبَّنَا ظَلَمْنَآ أَنْفُسَنَا وَإِن لَّم تَغفِرْ لَنَا وَتَرْحَمْنَا لَنَكُونَنَّ مِنَ
ٱلْخَٰسِرِينَ

Rabbanā ẓalamnā anfusanā wa-in lam taghfirlanā wa-tarḥamnā la-nakūnanna mina l-khāsirīn.

'Our Lord, we have wronged our souls: if You do not forgive us and have mercy upon us, we shall be lost.'

رَبِّ ٱجْعَلْنِي مُقِيمَ ٱلصَّلَوٰةِ وَمِنْ ذُرِّيَّتِي، رَبَّنَا وَتَقَبَّل دُعَآءِ،
رَبَّنَا ٱغْفِرْ لِي وَلِوَٰلِدَيَّ وَلِلْمُؤْمِنِينَ يَومَ يَقُومُ ٱلْحِسَابُ

Rabbi jʿalnī muqīma ṣ-ṣalāti wa-min dhurriyyatī rabbanā wa-taqabbal duʿā, Rabbanā ghfirlī wa-li-wālidayya wa-lil-muʾminīna yawm yaqūmu l-ḥisāb.

'Lord, grant that I and my offspring may keep up the prayer. Our Lord, accept my request. Our Lord, forgive me, my parents and the believers on the Day of Reckoning.'

اللَّهُمَّ إِنِّي أَعُوذُ بِكَ مِنْ عَذَابِ الْقَبْرِ، وَأَعُوذُ بِكَ مِنْ فِتْنَةِ الْمَسِيحِ الدَّجَّالِ، وَأَعُوذُ بِكَ مِنْ فِتْنَةِ المَحْيَا وفِتْنَةِ المَمَاتِ، اللَّهُمَّ إِنِّي أَعُوذُ بِكَ مِنَ المَأْثَمِ والمَغْرَمِ

Allāh-humma innī aʿūdhu bi-ka min ʿadhābi l-qabr, wa-aʿūdhu bi-ka min fitnati l-masīḥ d-dajjāl, wa-aʿūdhu bi-ka min fitnati l-maḥyā wa-fitnati l-mamāt. Allāh-humma innī aʿūdhu bi-ka mina l-ma'thami wa-l-maghram.

'O Allah, I seek refuge in You from the punishment of the grave, and I seek refuge in You from the trial of the Antichrist, and I seek refuge in You from the trials of this life and the hereafter. O Allah, I seek refuge in You from sin and debt.'

THE QUNŪT SUPPLICATION

اللَّهُمَّ إِنَّا نَسْتَعِينُكَ وَنَسْتَغْفِرُكَ وَنَتُوبُ إِلَيْكَ، وَنُؤْمِنُ بِكَ وَنَتَوَكَّلُ عَلَيْكَ، وَنُثْنِي عَلَيْكَ الخَيْرَ، نَشْكُرُكَ ولَا نَكْفُرُكَ، وَنَخْلَعُ وَنَتْرُكُ مَن يَفْجُرُكَ، اللَّهُمَّ إِيَّاكَ نَعْبُدُ وَلَكَ نُصَلِّي وَنَسْجُدُ، وَإِلَيْكَ نَسْعَى وَنَحْفِدُ، نَرْجُوا رَحْمَتَكَ وَنَخْشَى عَذَابَكَ، إِنَّ عَذَابَكَ الجِدَّ بِالْكُفَّارِ مُلْحِقٌ

Allāh-humma innā nastaʿīnuka wa-nastaghfiruka wa-natūbu ilayk(a), nu'minu bi-ka wa-natawakkalu ʿalayk(a), wa-nuthnī ʿalayka l-khayr(a), nashkuruka wa-lā nakfuruk(a), wa-nakhlaʿu wa-natruku man yafjurak(a), Allāh-humma iyyāka naʿbudu wa-laka nuṣallī wa-nasjud(u), wa-ilayka nasʿā wa-naḥfid(u), narjū raḥmataka wa-nakhshā ʿadhābak(a), inna ʿadhābaka l-jidda bi-l-kuffāri mulḥiq.

'O Allah, we seek Your succour and forgiveness and turn to You in repentance. We believe in You and have reliance upon

You. We praise You with good praise. We are thankful to You and are not ungrateful to You [and Your favours]. We abandon and leave anyone who disobeys You. O Allah, it is You whom we worship, and to You alone we pray and prostrate, and to You alone we strive and hasten. We have hope in Your mercy and fear Your punishment. Verily, Your true punishment will [certainly] be inflicted on the disbelievers.'

Bibliography

Abū Dāwūd al-Sijistānī, Sulaymān b. al-Ash'ath. *Sunan Abī Dāwūd*. 7 vols. Edited by Shu'ayb al-Arna'ūṭ and Muḥammad Kāmil Balalī. Beirut: Dār al-Risāla al-'Ālamiyya, 1430/2009.

Abūl-Ḥājj, Ṣalāḥ Muḥammad. *Minnat al-Fattāḥ 'alā Marāqī al-Falāḥ*. 3 vols. Beirut: Dār al-Bashā'ir al-Islāmiyya, 1437/2016.

Abūl-Ḥājj, Ṣalāḥ Muḥammad. *al-Mirqāt Sharḥ Muqaddimat al-Salāh*. Amman: Dār al-Fatḥ, 1439/2018.

'Āmūh, Muḥammad Aḥmad. *al-Ta'līqa al-Tihāmiyya 'alā al-Khulāṣa al-Kaydāniyya*. Hudayda: Dār Abī Ḥanīfa, 1437/2016.

Aṣfahānī, Abū Nu'aym Aḥmad b. 'Abdullāh al-. *Ḥilyat al-Awliyā' wa-Ṭabl aqāt al-Aṣfiyā'*. 10 vols. Beirut: Dār al-Fikr, 1416/1996.

'Asqalānī, Ibn Ḥajar al-. *al-Talkhīṣ al-Ḥabīr fī Takhrīj al-Aḥādīth al-Rāfi'ī al-Kabīr*. 4 vols. Beirut: Dār al-Kutub al-'Ilmiyya, 1419/1989.

'Aynī, Maḥmūd b. Aḥmad Badr al-Dīn al-. *Minḥat al-Sulūk Sharḥ Tuḥfat al-Mulūk*. Edited by Aḥmad al-Kubaysī. Syria, Lebanon, Kuwait: Dār al-Nawādir, 1432/2011.

Bājūrī, Ibrāhīm al-. *Tuḥfat al-Murīd 'alā Jawharat al-Tawḥīd*. Edited by 'Alī Jumu'a. Cairo: Dār al-Salām, 1433/2012.

Bukhārī, 'Abd al-'Azīz b. Aḥmad al-. *Kashf al-Asrār Sharḥ Uṣūl al-Bazdawī*. 4 vols. N.p.: Dār al-Kitāb al-Islāmī, n.d.

Bukhārī, Muḥammad b. Ismā'īl al-. *Ṣaḥīḥ al-Bukhārī*. 7 vols in 1. Edited by Muṣṭafā Dīb al-Bughā. Damascus: Dār Ibn Kathīr; Beirut: Yamāma, 1414/1993.

Bukhārī, Muḥammad b. Ismāʿīl al-. *Ṣaḥīḥ al-Bukhārī*. 9 vols. Edited by Muḥammad Zuhayr b. Nāṣir al-Nāṣir. Beirut: Dār Ṭūq al-Najāt, 1422/2001.

Dhahabī, Shams al-Dīn al-. *al-ʿIbar fī Khabar min Ghabar*. 4 vols. Edited by Muḥammad Zaghlūl. Beirut: Dār al-Kutub al-ʿIlmiyya, 1405/1985.

Ḥājjī Khalīfa [Muṣṭafā b. ʿAbdullāh]. *Kashf al-Ẓunūn ʿan Asāmī al-Kutub wa-l-Funūn*. 2 vols. Baghdad: Maktabat al-Muthannā, 1360/1941.

Ḥalabī, Ibrāhīm al-. *Ghunyat al-Mutamallī fī Sharḥ Munyat al-Muṣallī*. Durr Saʿādat, 1325/1907.

Ḥaṣkafī, ʿAlāʾ al-Dīn al-. *al-Durr al-Mukhtār Sharḥ Tanwīr al-Abṣār wa-Jāmiʿ al-Biḥār* [printed with *Radd al-Muḥtār*]. 12 vols. Edited by Muḥammad Ṣubhī Ḥasan Ḥallāq and ʿĀmir Ḥusayn. Beirut: Dār Iḥyāʾ al-Turāth al-ʿArabī, 1419/1998.

Ibn ʿĀbidīn, Muḥammad Amīn b. ʿUmar. *Nasamāt al-Asḥār ʿalā Sharḥ al-Manār*. Karachi: Idārat al-Qurʾān wa-l-ʿUlūm al-Islāmiyya, 1418/1997.

Ibn ʿĀbidīn, Muḥammad Amīn b. ʿUmar. *Radd al-Muḥtār ʿalā al-Durr al-Mukhtār*. 12 vols. Edited by Muḥammad Ṣubḥī Ḥasan Ḥallāq and ʿĀmir Ḥusayn. Beirut: Dār Iḥyāʾ al-Turāth al-ʿArabī, 1418/1998.

Ibn ʿĀbidīn, Muḥammad Amīn b. ʿUmar. *Minḥat al-Khāliq ʿalā al-Baḥr al-Rāʾiq*. 9 vols. Edited by Zakariyyā ʿUmayrāt. Beirut: Dār al-Kutub al-ʿIlmiyya, 1434/2013.

Ibn Abī Shayba, Abū Bakr. *al-Kitāb al-Muṣannaf fī al-Aḥādīth wa-l-Āthār*. 7 vols. Edited by Kamāl Yūsuf al-Ḥūt. Riyadh: Maktabat al-Rushd, 1989/1409.

Ibn Ḥanbal, Aḥmad b. Muḥammad. *Musnad Aḥmad b. Ḥanbal*. Edited by Shuʿayb al-Arnaʾūṭ et al. Beirut: Muʾassasat al-Risāla, 1422/2001.

Ibn al-Humām, Kamāl al-Dīn Muḥammad b. ʿAbd al-Wāḥid. *Fatḥ al-Qadīr ʿalā al-Hidāya*. 10 vols. Cairo: Muṣṭafā al-Babī al-Ḥalabī, 1389/1970.

Ibn al-Humām, Kamāl al-Dīn Muḥammad b. ʿAbd al-Wāḥid. *Fatḥ al-Qadīr ʿalā al-Hidāya*. 10 vols. 1389/1970. Reprint. Beirut: Dār al-Fikr, 1389/1970.

Ibn Māja, Muḥammad b. Yazīd al-Qazwīnī. *Sunan Ibn Māja*. 2 vols. Edited by Muḥammad Fuʾād ʿAbd al-Bāqī. N.p.: Dār Iḥyāʾ al-Kutub al-ʿAraa biyya, n.d.

Ibn Nujaym, Sirāj al-Dīn 'Umar b. Ibrāhīm. *al-Nahr al-Fā'iq Sharḥ Kanz al-Daqā'iq*. 3 vols. Edited by Aḥmad 'Izzaw 'Ināya. Beirut: Dār al-Kutub al-'Ilmiyya, 1422/2002.

Ibn Nujaym, Zayn al-Dīn b. Ibrāhīm. *al-Baḥr al-Rā'iq Sharḥ Kanz al-Daqā'iq*. 9 vols. Edited by Aḥmad 'Izzaw 'Ināya. Beirut: Dār Iḥyā' al-Turāth al-'Arabī, 1436/2015.

Kasānī, 'Alā' al-Dīn Abū Bakr b. Mas'ūd al-. *Badā'i' al-Ṣanā'i' fī Tartīb al-Sharā'i'*. 7 vols. Beirut: Dār al-Kutub al-'Ilmiyya, 1406/1986.

Kāshgharī, Muḥammad b. Muḥammad al-. *Munyat al-Muṣallī wa-Ghunyat al-Mubtadī*. Turkey: Durr Sa'ādat, 1325/1907.

Laknawī, 'Abd al-Ḥayy al-. *Nuzhat al-Fikr fī Subḥat al-Dhikr*. Edited by Ṣalāḥ Abūl-Ḥājj. Amman: Dār al-Fatḥ, 1422/2001.

Laknawī, 'Abd al-Ḥayy al-. *'Umdat al-Ri'āya 'alā Sharḥ al-Wiqāya*. 7 vols. Edited by Ṣalāḥ Abūl-Ḥājj. Beirut: Dār al-Kutub al-'Ilmiyya, 1430/2009.

Mawṣilī, 'Abdullāh b. Mas'ūd al-. *al-Ikhtiyār li-Ta'līl al-Mukhtār*. 4 vols. Edited by Shu'ayb al-Arna'ūt et al. Beirut: al-Risāla al-'Ālamiyya, 1431/2010.

Mulla Jīwan, Aḥmad b. Abī Sa'īd al-. *Nūr al-Anwār fī Sharḥ al-Manār*. 2 vols. Edited by Fatḥī al-Khālidī, Maḥmūd al-'Ubaydī and Sālim al-Shamrī. Kirkuk: Maktabat Amīr; Damascus: Dār Nūr al-Ṣabāḥ, 1436/2015.

Muslim b. al-Ḥajjāj. *Ṣaḥīḥ Muslim*. 5 vols. Edited by Muḥammad Fu'ād 'Abd al-Bāqī. Beirut: Dār Iḥyā' al-Kutub al-'Arabiyya, 1412/1991.

Nābulsī, 'Abd al-Ghanī al-. *al-Jawhar al-Kullī Sharḥ 'Umdat al-Muṣallī*. Edited by Muḥammad al-Dulaymī. Beirut: Dār al-Kutub al-'Ilmiyya, 1428/2007.

Naḥlāwī, Khalīl b. 'Abd al-Qādir al-. *al-Durar al-Mubāḥa fī al-Ḥaẓr wa-l-Ibāḥa*. Edited by Muḥammad Sa'īd al-Burhānī. Damascus: al-Maṭba'a al-'Ilmiyya, 1407/1987.

Nasā'ī, Aḥmad b. Shu'ayb al-. *al-Mujtabā min al-Sunan* (*al-Sunan al-Ṣughrā*). 9 vols. Edited by 'Abd al-Fattāḥ Abū Ghudda. Aleppo: Maktabat al-Maṭbū'āt al-Islāmiyya, 1406/1986.

Qārī, Mulla 'Alī al-. *Fatḥ Bāb al-'Ināya bi-Sharḥ al-Nuqāya*. 3 vols. Edited by Muḥammad Tamīm and Haytham Tamīm. Beirut: Dār al-Arqam, n.d.

Quḍā'ī, Muḥammad b. Salāma al-. *Musnad al-Shihāb*. 2 vols. Edited by Ḥamdī b. 'Abd al-Majīd. Beirut: Mu'assasat al-Risāla, 1407/1986.

Rāzī al-Ḥanafī, Zayn al-Dīn Muḥammad b. Abī Bakr al-. *Tuḥfat al-Mulūk*. Edited by Ṣalāḥ Abūl-Ḥājj. Amman: Dār al-Fārūq, 1427/2006.

Sarakhsī, Shams al-A'imma Abū Bakr Muḥammad b. Aḥmad al-. *al-Mabsūṭ*. 12 vols. Edited by Samīr Muṣṭafā Rabāb. Beirut: Dār Iḥyā' al-Turāth al-'Arabī, n.d.

Shaykhī Zāda, 'Abd al-Raḥmān b. al-Shaykh Muḥammad. *Majma' al-Anhur fī Sharḥ Multaqā al-Abḥur fī Furū' al-Ḥanafiyya*. 4 vols. Beirut: Dār Iḥyā' al-Turāth al-'Arabī, 1422/2001.

Shurunbulālī, Ḥasan b. 'Ammār al-. *Marāqī al-Falāḥ Sharḥ Nūr al-Īḍāḥ*. 3 vols. Edited by Ṣalāḥ Abūl-Ḥājj. Beirut: Dār al-Bashā'ir al-Islāmiyya, 1437/2016.

Suyūṭī, Jalāl al-Dīn al-. *al-Jāmi' al-Ṣaghīr min Ḥadīth al-Bashīr al-Nadhīr* [published with *al-Taysīr bi-Sharḥ al-Jāmi' al-Ṣaghīr* by Munāwī]. 2 vols. Riyadh: Maktabat Imām al-Shāfi'ī, 1408/1988.

Ṭabarānī, Sulaymān b. Aḥmad al-. *al-Mu'jam al-Kabīr*. 25 vols. Edited by Ḥamdī b. 'Abd al-Majīd. Cairo: Maktabat Ibn Taymiyya, n.d.

Taftāzānī, Sa'd al-Dīn Mas'ūd b. 'Umar al-. *al-Talwīḥ 'alā al-Tawḍīḥ li-Matan al-Tanqīḥ*. 2 vols. Edited by Zakariyyā 'Umayrāt. Beirut: Dār al-Kutub al-'Ilmiyya, n.d.

Ṭaḥṭāwī, Aḥmad al-. *Ḥāshiyat al-Ṭaḥṭāwī 'alā Marāqī al-Falāḥ*. 2 vols. Edited by 'Abd al-Karīm al-'Aṭā'. Damascus: Dār Qubā, Dār Nūr al-Ṣabāḥ and Maktabat Amīr, 1436/2015.

Tumurtāshī, Muḥammad b. 'Abdullāh al-. *Tanwīr al-Abṣār wa-Jāmi' al-Biḥār* [printed with *Durr al-Mukhtār* and *Radd al-Mukhtār*]. 12 vols. Edited by Muḥammad Ṣubḥī Ḥasan Ḥallāq and 'Āmir Ḥusayn. Beirut: Dār Iḥyā' al-Turāth al-'Arabī, 1418/1998.

Tirmidhī, Muḥammad b. 'Īsā al-. *Sunan al-Tirmidhī*. 5 vols. Edited by Aḥmad Muḥammad Shākir, Muḥammad Fu'ād 'Abd al-Bāqī and Ibrāhīm 'Iwaḍ. Cairo: Muṣṭafā al-Bābī al-Ḥalabī, 1395/1975.

'Uthmānī, Muḥammad Taqī al-. *Uṣūl al-Iftā wa-Ādābuhū*. Damascus: Dār al-Qalam, 1435/2014.

Zaylaʿī, ʿUthmān b. ʿAlī-. *Tabyīn al-Ḥaqāʾiq Sharḥ Kanz al-Daqāʾiq*. 7 vols. Edited by Aḥmad ʿIzzaw ʿInāya. Beirut: Dār al-Kutub al-ʿIlmiyya, 1431/2010.

Zaylī, Abūl-Layth Muḥarram b. Muḥammad al-. *Hadiyyat al-Ṣaʿlūk Sharḥ Tuḥfat al-Mulūk*. Unpublished manuscript.

About the Translator

Siddiq Adam Mitha is the founder of Fiqhra, an educational platform for teaching and promoting traditional Islamic scholarship. Siddiq comes from Bolton in the north-west of England where he went through the traditional madrasa system and developed an initial thirst for studying Islam. His enthusiasm and abilities were well noted by teachers and peers alike. Later as an adult, Siddiq left Bolton and went to study medicine at the University of Liverpool. Here, he was active in the Islamic Society and through his role as president, he organised lessons and events for the Muslim student polity. He met inspiring teachers who further ignited his thirst for knowledge, and after completing medical school and the subsequent training, he decided to answer his heart's call and follow his lifelong passion for studying and teaching the sacred sciences. He has since spent several years studying in Amman, Jordan. During this time, he has studied the Arabic language, *ʿaqīda* (creed), *manṭiq* (logic), hadith sciences, *taṣawwuf* (Sufism) and is currently specialising in Ḥanafī fiqh and *uṣūl* (methodology) under the tutelage and guidance of Dr Ṣalāḥ Abūl-Ḥājj at the College of Ḥanafī Fiqh at the World Islamic Sciences and Education University. In addition, some of his other teachers include Shaykh ʿAlī Zayno, Shaykh Aḥmad al-Ḥasanāt, Shaykh ʿAbd al-Raḥmān al-Shaʿʿār, Shaykh ʿAlī Hānī, Shaykh Ismāʿīl al-Kurdī, Shaykh Muḥammad Nūr al-Ṣābirīn, Shaykh Muʿādh Ḥawwā, Ustādh Maḥmūd al-Shūrbajī and Dr Muḥammad al-Najjār. He currently resides with his family in Amman, Jordan, where he is continuing his studies, as well as researching and writing, contributing to the corpus of Islamic literature in the English-speaking world.